New complete guide of

VENICE

265 color illustrations
62 black and white drawings
Map of the city
Compendium of useful information

D0369841

BONECHI EDIZIONI "IL TURISMO" FIRENZE

Exclusive distributor for Venice:
BENEDETTI SOUVENIRS S.a.S. di Roberto Benedetti & C.
Via Cannaregio 3548/49
30121 VENICE
Phone +39 (41) 71.87.82-72.09.77 - Fax +39 (41) 52.40.767

THE PHOTOGRAPHS OF THE
WORKS INSIDE ST. MARK'S
BASILICA WERE MADE AVAILABLE
THROUGH THE COURTESY OF
THE PROCURATORIA DI SAN
MARCO DI VENEZIA

© Copyright 1997 by Bonechi Edizioni "Il Turismo" S.r.l
Via dei Rustici, 5 -50122 FLORENCE
Phone +39 (55) 239.82.24/25 - Fax +39 (55) 21.63.66
E-mail address: barbara@bonechi.com / bbonechi@dada.it
Printed in Italy

Black and white drawings: Claudia Baggiani
Photographs: The Bonechi Edizioni "Il Turismo" S.r.l. Archives
        Paolo Bacherini
        I-Buga S.a.s. Milan: p. 37 - p. 47 (Auth. SMA n.00034,
        22/04/1991) - p. 48 (Auth. SMA n.00347, 22/04/1991)
        p. 50 (Auth. SMA n.00480, 11/06/1991) -p. 178 (Auth. SMA
        n.00034, 22/04/1991) - p. 186 (Auth. SMA n.00480,
        11/06/1991) -p. 191 top (Auth. SMA n. 00480, 11/06/1991)
        p. 193 top (Auth. SMA n.00480 , 11/06/1991) - p. 195 top
        and bottom left (Auth. n.00480, 11/06/1991)
        Giorgio Deganello: pp. 71-73-74-75-76-77-78-79-81-82-83
Layout and cover design: Claudia Baggiani
Photolithography: La Fotolitografia, Florence
Printed by: Lito Terrazzi, Florence
ISBN 88-7204-265-8

We wish to express our special thanks to the **Peggy Guggenheim**
Collection *for the text and photographs on pages 181 - 182 - 183.*

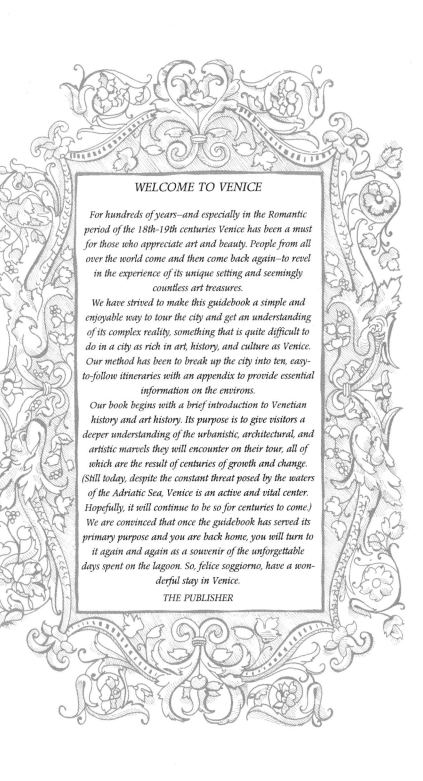

WELCOME TO VENICE

For hundreds of years–and especially in the Romantic period of the 18th-19th centuries Venice has been a must for those who appreciate art and beauty. People from all over the world come and then come back again–to revel in the experience of its unique setting and seemingly countless art treasures.

We have strived to make this guidebook a simple and enjoyable way to tour the city and get an understanding of its complex reality, something that is quite difficult to do in a city as rich in art, history, and culture as Venice. Our method has been to break up the city into ten, easy-to-follow itineraries with an appendix to provide essential information on the environs.

Our book begins with a brief introduction to Venetian history and art history. Its purpose is to give visitors a deeper understanding of the urbanistic, architectural, and artistic marvels they will encounter on their tour, all of which are the result of centuries of growth and change. (Still today, despite the constant threat posed by the waters of the Adriatic Sea, Venice is an active and vital center. Hopefully, it will continue to be so for centuries to come.) We are convinced that once the guidebook has served its primary purpose and you are back home, you will turn to it again and again as a souvenir of the unforgettable days spent on the lagoon. So, felice soggiorno, have a wonderful stay in Venice.

THE PUBLISHER

ART AND HISTORICAL OUTLINE

FROM THE 5th TO THE 15th CENTURIES

Around the middle of the 5th century A.D. the people from Aquileia, Caorle, Altinum, and other mainland cities fleeing the Barbarian invaders, sought refuge on the Islands dotting the Venetian lagoon. This was the earliest nucleus of the city that would one day be known as Venice. The new inhabitants of the lagoon soon set about governing themselves by instituting the so-called "Maritime Tribunes". The men to fill these positions were appointed by the Exarch of Ravenna who in turn was the representative of the Byzantine Emperor in Italy. In the 7th century, the institutions went through a major change when the Tribunes were replaced by dukes, or dogi. Though they were at first appointed by the Emperor, soon the evergrowing autonomy that the Venetians wrested from the central authority gave them the right to elect their own doges in popular assemblies. Despite the fact that Venice was soon free of the control of both Ravenna and Byzantium, her ties with the Byzantine world were far from severed and continued to play a major role in the city's economic, artistic, and cultural development.

In fact, for centuries Venice represented the main point of contact between East and West and, as such, the privileged hub in the interchanges between both worlds. The Basilica of Santa Maria Assunta, built in 639 on the island of Torcello in pure Ravennate style, is testimony of the first period of strong bonds with Ravenna, the Byzantine capital of the West.

At the beginning of the 11th century, Venice was invaded by the army led by Pepin, King of the Franks, but she withstood the attack and was able to preserve her autonomy. Following the Treaty of Aix-la-Chapelle (812) which sanctioned Venice's subordination—actually more formal than otherwise—to Byzantium, the city was able to expand her activities on sea and land through both military and diplomatic actions. At the same time, the Venetians went about consolidating their government institutions: the powers and duties of the doge were codified, while public office was awarded within an ever-narrowing circle of aristocrats.

The effects of greatly-increased trade and thus greater availability of capital were also physically evident in the appearance of the city which soon begin to fill up with new churches and palaces. One of the new churches, in fact, was the St. Mark's Basilica (832) built to house the mortal remains of the Evangelist Mark. Throughout this period the major stylistic influence came from Ravenna.

5

During the 10th, 11th, and 12th centuries, Venice strengthened her dominion over the Dalmatian and Istrian coasts, defeated the Normans, her rivals for the subjugation of the Adriatic, and, demonstrating great skill as a mediator, was able to benefit from the fierce struggles between the Emperor and Communes.

During this time the Romanesque style was developing and taking root all over Europe. Romanesque in Venice acquired a special quality, since it blended with Byzantine and Moorish elements. The most splendid example of architecture of the time was the grandiose St. Mark's Basilica (1063) adorned with marble and gold which in the subsequent centuries would be further enriched by Gothic art. This period, too, saw the first aristocratic palaces rise along the Grand Canal with their ground floor fondachi (warehouses) for the flourishing trading activities. Venice's participation in the Crusades could hardly be termed constant. At first, the Crusade called by Urban II in 1095 was regarded with suspicion by the Venetians who feared that trade with the Orient could be negatively affected. Later, though, Venice drew considerable benefits, both political and commercial, from the Crusades, especially the fourth one sponsored by Innocent III.

In fact, Doge Enrico Dandolo, the real founder of the maritime power of the Repubblica della Serenissima, as Venice came to be called, adhered to the undertaking and managed it in such a way that Venice drew great advantages from the Crusade. The Byzantine territories of Zara (1202), Durazzo, several islands of the Aegean, Peloponnesus, Crete and still others were conquered and annexed.

This was the period of Venice's maximum development as a sea power, of Marco Polo's travels in the Far East, and the importation and widespread diffusion of raw materials and manufactured goods from the Orient throughout Europe. Once more the city adjusted its governing bodies to the new situation. After the creation of the Procuratori di San Marco whose tasks involved public administration, the two councils were set up—the Maggior Consiglio (Greater Council) in 1172 and the Consiglio Piccolo (Small Council) in 1178—to help the doge rule the extensive Venetian territories. In 1179 the Tribunale Supremo della Quarantia, the supreme court of the Republic, was established, soon followed by the so-called "Pregadi", which were committees composed of the most influential citizens whose job it was to help the doge and councils govern.

In 1297 the "Serrata del Maggior Consiglio" (Closure) brought in new legislative dispositions which assured the nobles once and for all that they would have permanent access to all political appointments including the dogeship.

This series of reforms caused fierce internecine fighting amongst the various Venetian factions. In 1310 a conspiracy led by the Querini-Tiepolo families brought about the exile of Tiepolo and the creation of the famous Council of Ten for national security. This council became so powerful that it even passed the death sentence on a doge, Marin Faliero, who was charged with high treason when he tried to make himself absolute ruler of the Republic.

During the Gothic period, Venetian architecture retained certain characteristics that would never change. These features give Venice its unique appearance buildings of various periods all exude a similar feeling of delicate airiness, which is the effect conveyed by the pastel colors and lacy façades pierced by mullioned windows and edged with crenellation. The Gothic period was the time when Moorish influence was at its apex. Starting in the early 1200s and through the first half of the 15th century, a unique version of the International Gothic

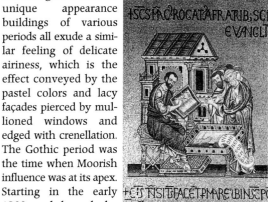

St. Mark Writing
(Zen Chapel).

Style developed in Venetian architecture. Outstanding examples are the Doges' Palace and the Ca' d'Oro. Another art form, mosaics, reached great splendor in Venice. The early ones, still very much influenced by the Byzantine mosaics of Ravenna, became jewel-like paintings in the hands of the West's most skilled craftsmen, the Venetian mosaicists. The finest examples can still be seen in St. Mark's and

the Cathedral of Torcello. In Medieval Venetian painting, Byzantine influence predominated more than anywhere else on the Italian peninsula. In the 14th century, however, Venetian painters such as Paolo Veneziano and Guariento receptive to the innovations the Florentine Giotto had brought to painting, began to shed the stylistic restrictions imposed by the Byzantine style. By the 15th century Jacobello del Fiore and Michele Giambono had achieved a successful blend of the Byzantine and the International Style. Moreover, Venice always held an important position in the so-called "minor arts", glassblowing (in Murano), woodcarving, and the crafting of wrought iron. Venice's expansionist policy, which had brought great prosperity to her citizens, encountered its first serious setback with the rise of a rival, the Republic of Genoa. The struggle between the two sea powers for supremacy of the Mediterranean lasted over a hundred years, starting from the first skirmish in 1277 up to the Treaty of Turin of 1381. Nor did Venice have an easy time defending her mainland territories. The struggle she waged against Filippo Maria Visconti, Duke of Brescia and Bergamo, was long and hard, but the Venetians, commanded by Doge Francesco Foscari, finally won and peace was sanctioned under the Treaty of Cremona of 1441. Shortly after, however, the war flared up again when Visconti was succeeded by Francesco Sforza and did not end until 1454 when the Treaty of Lodi, which established a relatively stable equilibrium amongst Venice, Milan and Florence, was signed.

In the 15th century Venice's economic and political supremacy showed the first signs of crisis, mainly due to the rise of the Turks as a Mediterranean sea power. Actually, previous relations between Turkey and Venice were relatively friendly, both economically and politically speaking. Without warning, however, in 1416 the Moslems overran and sacked Eubea and the Cyclades Islands, both territories belonging to the Repubblica di San Marco. The Venetians immediately retaliated and Doge Pietro Loredan inflicted a terrible blow upon the Turkish fleet. The Turks, however, refused to give up without a fight and proceeded to attack Thessalonica.

Faced with the prospect of a long drawn-out war, the Venetians decided it would be wiser to negotiate peace with the Ottoman sovereign, Mohammed II, who nevertheless failed to keep his side of the bargain and soon war broke out once more.

The struggle dragged on and on causing great hardships on Venice whose territories of Argos, Negropont, Corone, and Lepanto fell to the Turks and whose position of supremacy on the Mediterranean—the basis of Venetian fame and fortune—was seriously threatened. The culminating episode of the whole war was the Battle of Navarrino (1499), which was disastrous for both of the contending fleets. Venice's outlook brightened somewhat in 1489 when she acquired Cyprus as a result of the marriage of a Venetian noblewoman, Caterina Corner, to the king of the island James II, but a few years later, in 1503, she was forced into stipulating an onerous peace treaty which deprived her of a big chunk of Morea.

In 1438 the Venetian fleet was soundly beaten at Prevesa and again in 1570, despite the heroic defense put up by Admiral Marcantonio Bragadin, the capital of Cyprus, Famagosta, fell into the hands of the attacking Turks. At this point the Christian world decided to put a halt to the Turkish advance and joined together in an alliance which included Spain, Savoy, the Knights of Malta, and the Vatican State. The decisive battle was fought in 1571 off the coast of Lepanto and resulted in a stunning victory for the Christians. Yet the situation hardly improved: the allied league split up, the Turks continued to make attacks, and Venice ended up ceding Cyprus under a treaty stipulated in

1573. At that point little was left of the once great sea power's former supremacy. In addition, competition from other nations, mainly Spain and Portugal, favored by the opening of new trade routes with the Indies and growing importations from the Americas, made inroads on Venice's commercial dominion.

From an artistic standpoint the period during which the Renaissance was born and developed, first in Tuscany, then throughout Italy, found Venice still clinging to the elaborate style of the Late Gothic. Then, when the Renaissance style finally managed to manifest itself, it immediately became mixed in with the local style, so that the result was a combination of Renaissance and the Byzantine Gothic style the Venetians had favored for centuries. New motifs came into Venetian sculpture in the mid 1400s with the arrival of Pietro Lombardo and his sons, architects and sculptors, while in painting, years earlier, Paolo Uccello and Andrea del Castagno, two of the foremost Early Renaissance painters from Florence, had brought the new style to the lagoon city. Just a few years later, Andrea Mantegna arrived from Padua and formed a circle of artists, the most famous of whom were Carpaccio and the Bellini family. The 16th century was a period of exceptional splendor for Venetian painting, which in fact had an enormous influence on all of Italian art. Giorgione, Titian, Lorenzo Lotto, Veronese, and Tintoretto are some of the names which give an idea of the importance of the 16th century Venetian masters. Also, in the 1500s the city was embellished with grandiose architectural creations, mainly due to the efforts of

The Miraculous Cure of the Possessed Man, by *Vittore Carpaccio*
(Gallery of the Accademia).

The church of San Giorgio Maggiore.

Opposite page: ***Procession in St. Mark's Square,*** by *Gentile Bellini* (Galleria dell'Accademia).

The church of Santa Maria della Salute.

Antonio Rizzo (who, for example, designed the east wing of the Doges' Palace) and Jacopo Sansovino (architect of the Libreria di San Marco and the Loggetta by the Belltower in Piazza San Marco, among others).

During the 16th-17th centuries, two other great architects, Andrea Palladio (the churches of the Redentore and San Giorgio Maggiore) and Baldassarre Longhena (church of Santa Maria della Salute) left their mark on the distinctive Venetian cityscape. The disastrous warring with the Turks also had an indirect effect on Venice's mainland policy. After having made several attempts to conquer new territories from her neighbors at the beginning of the 16th century, which led to growing hostility from the major Italian powers, Venice, hemmed in on all sides, was forced to act a bit more wisely, tempering her actions with a good dose of prudence as well. Throughout the 16th and 17th centuries she limited her territorial claims and reduced her military actions to defending her own territories. In 1669 she was even forced to surrender the island of Crete to the Turks, whereby she was left with only a tiny part of her once extensive Mediterranean possessions.

The expansionist aims of the great European powers, mainly Austria, threatened her independence time and time again. In the 18th century her territory was overrun numerous times during the war of succession fought

amongst Spain, Poland, and Austria, and Venice was unable to intervene in any way. By the end of the 18th century, the old aristocratic Venetian constitution, threatened by the spread of the new social ideas sparked by the French Revolution, could no longer resist and was discarded. In 1797, under the Treaty of Campoformio, Napoleon handed Venice and her territories to Austria, bringing to an end a long tradition of independence and institutional continuity that had no equal in the history of the Italian peninsula.

Although the 18th century was for Venice a period of decline in many ways, the city remained a hub of artistic activity— this was the heyday of famous painters such as Piazzetta, Carriera, Tiepolo, Canaletto, Guardi, and Pietro Longhi and sculptors such as Antonio Canova. In the 19th century Venice tried to rid herself of Austrian domination. Under the leadership of Daniele Manin, many Venetians took part in the uprisings of 1848 in the Risorgimento movement for Italian unity. Their efforts were crowned with success when, after a favorable plebiscite, Venice was annexed to the Kingdom of Italy in 1866. From 1866 to the present day, Venice has maintained her position as an art center and site of international art exhibits (the most important of which, the Biennale, was first held in 1895) and as a hub of international tourism which has become one of the city's major economic resources. Venice also has an active industrial zone, in the mainland suburbs of Marghera and Mestre.

In June 1979 the inhabitants of Venice, Marghera, and Mestre, called to vote on whether they should remain under the same township or separate, cast their ballots in favor of remaining united, just as they have been for centuries.

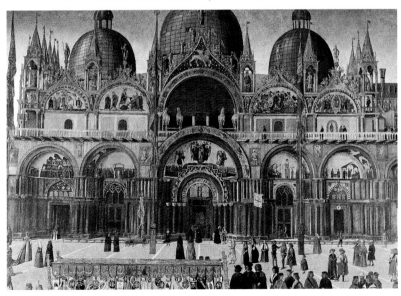

FOUNDATIONS RESTING ON PILES

A unique feature of Venetian buildings.

In the fifth century, the inhabitants of the northern Adriatic coast took flight before the barbarian tribes sweeping down over Italy and decided to settle the lagoon islands–this is the origin of the city later to be known as Venice. One of their first difficulties was constructing dwellings that would be safe from the frequent floods the area was subject to, and this problem was probably overcome by the use of tree-trunk piles. Thereafter, as the buildings became more and more complex, stone and brick replaced wood as the main building material. Nevertheless, it was impossible to avoid the use of supports and still today the foundations of Venetian buildings rise upon countless piles sunk into the muddy depths of the lagoon. That architectural marvels such as the St. Mark's Basilica, the Rialto Bridge, and the Belltower required hundreds of thousands of these piles to sustain them is truly incredible. Thus, we can say that Venice actually rests upon a forest of tree-trunks, mostly larchwood (This wood is fortunately quite rugged and highly resistant to the water).

Sectional view of the north side of the Campanile and the Loggetta.
The piles sunken into the ground to support the weight of the structures are visible at the bottom.

FLOODS IN VENICE

The phenomenon of high tides (called "acqua alta" or high water in Venetian) is such a common experience that the Venetians have come to accept them philosopically, without any big fuss. The water seems to have a special fondness for Piazza San Marco and the church, where it can get more than 11/2 feet deep so that, it is possible to see a gondola navigating on the square or even beneath the arches.

ARCHITECTURAL STYLES IN VENICE

  Touring Venice, we soon realize that the buildings can be grouped into four major categories of architectural styles. Each of them (Byzantine, Romanesque, Gothic and Renaissance) is typical of a period. Below we have briefly outlined their main characteristics.

  The Byzantine style - *This style abounds in ornamentation, precious materials, and dynamic forms, especially stressed by the use of arches and domes. The Byzantine dome is either sustained by four or eight columns (four if the shape is square, eight if it is octagonal) connected by arches. An essential feature of the Byzantine church are the columns, grouped to form galleries, that support the domes. The capitals, adorned with acanthus leaf and animal patterns, are usually topped with carved entablatures. The walls and ceilings are covered with rich mosaics. Although this style flourished mainly from the 6th to 12th centuries, it left its imprint on all periods of Venetian art.*

The Romanesque style - *This style spread all over Christendom during the early Middle Ages. It appeared in Venice as an offshoot of the Byzantine style towards the 11th-12th centuries. Romanesque churches are easily recognizable with their thick stone walls pierced by tiny windows. Inside, a double row of columns joined by round arches divides the nave from the aisles. The ceiling is often beamed.*

The Gothic style - *The label "Gothic" dates from the Renaissance period, since the Italian Renaissance artists deemed Gothic art inferior to the* purity of the art of Antiquity; for them "Gothic" was synonomous with barbarian (Goths). The style developed in Northern France in the 12th century. In Italy, and in particular in Venice, it flourished from the 12th through 15th centuries. Its main features are pointed arches, soaring yet airy elevations (in fact everything seems to be striving towards the sky), buttresses, and enormous windows divided into two or more zones by columns (the so-called mullioned windows) adorned with carved upper parts.

The Ca' d'Oro.

The Renaissance style - *This is the style that, starting from the 15th century, signified the Italian artists' striving for a rebirth (rinascita) of the Antique, and, in fact, the Renaissance artists were inspired by Greek and Roman masterpieces which they adapted to the needs and tastes of their own times. The main features of the Renaissance style are plain columns, round arches, use of friezes, cornices, trabeations and other Classical motifs, coffered ceilings either painted or carved, rectangular windows adorned with elaborate cornices resting on pilasters or columns, and richness of ornamentation. With the advent of the Baroque style in the 17th century, this richness becomes increasingly grandiose, until the straight line is almost completely supplanted by the curved line.*

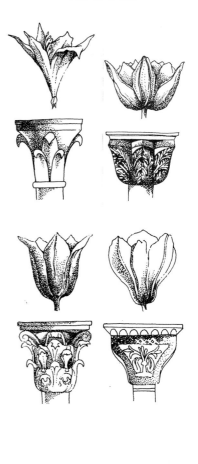

Rio del Cristo; opposite: *Rio di San Maurizio*; below: *Rio del Tentor.*

THE RIOS OF VENICE

The city is crisscrossed by hundreds of waterways called "rii" (plural of rio). The fact that these picturesque canals are all different lends them a special charm. The Rio di San Barnaba is a busy thorough for barges and cargo vessels. A tree-shaded little square overlooks the Rio di San Vio; Rio del Malpaga is silent and solitary, while the Rio del Vin flows along the Riva degli Schiavoni.

Two typical "rii" in the heart of Venice.

THE LA FENICE THEATER

La Fenice is the most important theater in Venice, indeed it is one of the most important opera houses in Italy. The building (like so many others in the city) was burned down in fires which broke out several times. In fact, its name Fenice (phoenix), comes from the fact that each time, just like the mythical bird, it was reborn from its very ashes. Rebuilt at the end of the 18th century, it is now one of the city's most vital artistic and cultural centers.

The interior of La Fenice before the last fire in 1996.

VENETIAN CUISINE

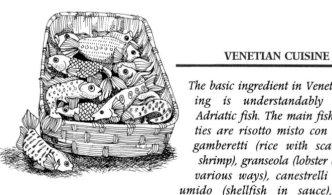

The basic ingredient in Venetian cooking is understandably excellent Adriatic fish. The main fish specialities are risotto misto con scampi e gamberetti (rice with scampi and shrimp), granseola (lobster cooked in various ways), canestrelli in umido (shellfish in sauce), folpetto all'olio or al limone (polyps with oil or lemon), seppie (cuttlefish), and baccala mantecato (cod in a white sauce). Non-fish specialities include pasta e fagioli (a thick bean soup with noodles), risi e biri (rice with peas), fegato alla veneziana (calves' liver and onions), and trippa alla venetiana (tripe, Venetian style).

*A picturesque view of the historical regatta
on the Grand Canal.*

THE REGATA STORICA

The custom of holding regattas in Venice, while rooted in the past, is still very much alive today. Of all the races, the best known and most spectacular and, judging from the participation, the most popular – is the Regata Storica (historic boat race) which is held the first Sunday of September. The idea of holding a race of this kind has always been attributed to Doge Giovanni Soranzo (1315), although the regatta as we see it today dates from a personal initiative of Mayor Filippo Grimani in 1896.

THE CARNEVALE DI VENEZIA

The word Carnevale comes from the Latin "Carnen levare", that is, take away the flesh and has always signified the festive period between Christmas and Lent. Customarily the Carnevale begins on 17 January the feast of St. Anthony Abbot, even though the actual celebrations take place on the last three days. In the past the Carnevale reached its maximum splendor in Venice when the Doge, the Signoria, the Senate and the Ambassadors participated in the popular feast of Carnival Thursday, the last Thursday before Lent. It was celebrated by the burning of a bull, a man's "flight" along a wire stretched between the Campanile and the Doge's Palace, and fireworks.

Over the past few years the Carnevale celebrations have taken on renewed vigor. Thousands of visitors from all over the world flock to St. Mark's Square, the world's most beautiful salon to show off their costumes in a spirit of carefree gaiety.

FIRST ITINERARY

E veryone who drives to Venice has to park in the **Piazzale Roma**, which is the huge parking lot and bus temminal for the buses linking the city to the mainland towns. The Piazzale is connected to the mainland by the **Ponte della Libertà** erected in 1933 alongside the 1876 railway bridge. The building of the bridge and Piazzale was made necessary by the impelling need to facilitate both cargo and tourist connections with the

The imbarcadero, the vaporetto, "water bus", stop near the station.

mainland. Turning our backs on Piazzale Roma, we are now ready to enter the heart of the city by way of its main "thoroughfare", the **Grand Canal**. The most widely-used means of getting around in Venice is the vaporetto (water bus). Vaporetto service along the Grand Canal dates back to 1881. Proceeding along the **Rio Nuovo** and the **Papadopoli Gardens** we reach the **Pontile di Santa Chiara** (embarking station) on the **Fondamenta Santa Chiara** where we take a vaporetto for a scenic ride along the Grand Canal.

The Santa Lucia railroad station.

21

THE GRAND CANAL

The Grand Canal, shaped like a huge upside down "S" bisecting the city, is almost 2$^{1/2}$miles long, 15 feet deep, and ranges from about 100 to 225 feet across. Its aqueous "paving" sparkles in the sunlight, although the water is sometimes wave-capped and can even become sombre and menacing, depending on the weather and the season. Flanking the canal on either side is a parade of incredible buildings, brightly colored little houses alongside imposing stone palaces, dating from every period and exemplifying every architectural style. Even the most distracted sightseer cannot help but be enthralled by the vision of charming buildings, squares, tiny canals extending into the shadows, gardens stolen from the threatening grasp of the sea, and a lovely gateway here and there, blackened and corroded by the weather and the water. It is no wonder that painters and poets, musicians and writers have always expressed such great admiration for the canal. Byron, Canova, Wagner, Hemingway, among hundreds of others, all spent lengthy periods of their lives on or near its banks.

The Grand Canal.

View of the Grand Canal; below: *the Santa Lucia railroad station.*

Immediately to our left we note the **Santa Lucia Station**. The railway station was named after the Palladian church dedicated to St. Lucy originally on the site, which was torn down in the middle of the 19th century to make way for the railroad linking Venice to the mainland. The railway bridge, officially inaugurated in 1846 was quite an engineering feat itself: 225 spans are supported by 75,00 pylons anchored in the depths of the lagoon. On the other hand, the station is actually a recent construction opened to the public in 1954.

The church of San Simeone Piccolo.

From the station, proceeding in the direction of St. Mark's, we immediately note the attractive **church of San Simeone Piccolo** (also called San Simeone e Giuda) just to right of the station building. The most striking part of the church is its huge copper dome and lantern, surmounted by a statue of *Christ the Redeemer*, whose distinctive green color is due to the effects of weathering.

The church dominates the whole first stretch of the Grand Canal, with its impressive staircase leading down to the water. Framing the entrance is an 18th century neo-Classical porch with Corinthian columns, designed by Giovanni Scalfarotto. The majestic gable crowning it is adorned with *Scenes of the Martyrdom of Saints Simeon and Judas* sculpted by Francesco Penso.

The first bridge we encounter on our way to St. Mark's is the **Ponte degli Scalzi**, also known as the Station Bridge. Made entirely of white Istrian stone, it was designed by Eugenio Miozzi and put up in 1934 to replace a metal structure built in 1858 by the Lombard-Venetian city administration. The single span bridge is approximately 130 feet long and rises approximately 23 feet above water level. On the left bank by the bridge we note the imposing Baroque façade of the **church of Santa Maria di Nazareth** (or Santa Maria degli Scalzi).

The church of Santa Maria di Nazareth; below: *the Ponte degli Scalzi on the Grand Canal.*

Keeping our eyes riveted to the left side, our gaze encounters the apse and belfry of the **church of San Geremia** which was first built in the 13th century and later remodeled in 1760. Its Romanesque belltower dates back to the 13th century and is thus one of the oldest in the city. Alongside the church is a grandiose 18th century patrician palace, the **Palazzo Labia** whose interior was frescoed by Tiepolo. On the far corner is a *statue of St. John Nepomucenus* commissioned by one of the ladies of the Labia family. Still keeping our eyes to the left, just beyond the statue of the saint we see the beginning of the **Cannaregio Canal**, the second largest in Venice after the Grand Canal. Further on, this time on the right, is one of the most celebrated buildings in the Venetian Byzantine style, the **Fondaco dei Turchi**. The building was totally (and very arbitrarily) remodeled in the 19th century on the site of the 12th-13th century palace which was once the

Preceding page, from above: *the Ponte delle Guglie on the Canale di Cannaregio; the church of San Geremia, façade, and a view from the Grand Canal.*

The Canale di Cannaregio; below: *the Fondaco dei Turchi.*

headquarters and trade center of the Oriental merchants stationed in Venice. Today it is the **Museum of Natural History**.

Once we have passed the **Rio della Maddalena** we encounter on the left **Palazzo Vendramin Calergi**, an outstanding example of Renaissance architecture. Begun by Coducci and completed by Lombardo in 1509, it was where Richard Wagner died on February 13, 1883. A series of fine palaces follows. The first is the 17th century **Palazzo Ruoda,** with its completely remodeled façade. Just beyond we note the 16th century **Palazzo Gussoni-Grimani della Vida** attributed to Sanmicheli. Originally a fresco by Tintoretto adorned its façade, but like all other outdoor murals in Venice, this one too, corroded by brine and weathering, has been lost to us. Next we see the **Palazzetto Da Lezze** with its tiny façade overgrown with vines, the 17th century **Palazzo Boldù** with its rusticated stone groundfloor, and lastly the **Palazzo Contarini-Pisani,** 17th century as well, with its spacious portico on the canal side.

Palazzo Vendramin Calergi.

Palazzo Barbarigo.

Palazzo Belloni-Battagia.

Opposite these buildings is the majestic **Ca' Pesaro** acclaimed as Baldassarre Longhena's masterpiece of privately-commissioned architecture, and built between 1679 and 1710. So great did the building costs seem at the time that the architect is said to have died from worrying about whether the project would ever be finished. The imposing façade rises upon a rusticated stone base surmounted by a double tier of windows set off by clusters of columns. The building today houses the **International Gallery of Modern Art** and the **Oriental Art Museum.** On the same side, right by the Ca' Pesaro, is the **Palazzo Corner della Regina**, a Classical style building designed by Domenico Rossi (1724) on the site of the pre-existing Palazzo Cornaro. Today it is the headquarters of a banking organization.

Palazzo Corner della Regina.
Opposite page:
Ca' Pesaro.

rising out of the Grand Canal.

On the ground floor is a portico which, except for the central round arch, is composed of graceful pointed arches. The two upper floors have delicately pierced loggias. The righthand section of the façade is more compact with fewer empty spaces, but it is in no way less elegant than the left side. Surmounting the façade is a crown of finely wrought crenellation.

On the left is another palace, the **Palazzo Sagredo**, a late 14th century Gothic building, with an elaborate façade. Across the canal, we cannot help but notice a two storey brick structure jutting out a bit from the other buildings. This is the **Pescheria**, or Fish Market which was built in 1907 by Domenico Rupolo after a design by the painter Cesare Laurenti. It opens on the Grand Canal by means of a spacious portico of slightly-pointed arches resting on columns which support a slanting roof to form the huge open loggia.

Continuing along the left, we soon reach the most celebrated of the many remarkable buildings lining the Grand Canal, the **Ca' d'Oro**. After having been remodeled time and time again (and not always wisely) and passed from owner to owner, it came into the possession of Baron Giorgio Franchetti who in 1916 donated the palace along with the art collection bearing his name to the Italian state. The façade, which today is white, was originally gilded and this gave it its name - Ca' d'Oro, in fact, means Golden House. Built around 1440 for a nobleman, Marino Contarini, in a style which combines Byzantine influence with the Gothic pointed arch motifs, it looks like charming lace embroidery

The Pescheria.

The building rises on the site of what has always been Venice's fish market, although this particular version was built to replace a metal structure erected in the 19th century when a still earlier one was torn down.

The Rialto Fish Market, as it is called was the most important of the many fish markets that once dotted the city. A *statue of St. Peter*, whom Christ called a "fisher of men", stands on one side of the building.

Preceding page: *the Ca' d'Oro.*

Palazzo Foscari and Palazzo Michiel dalle Colonne seen from the Pescheria.

On the opposite side of the canal once more, we can make out the **Palazzo Michiel dalle Colonne** with its distinctive ground floor colonnade. The denomination "of the Columns" is thought by some to derive from these very columns, whereas others believe it was added to the Michiel name because it was a member of the family who actually brought the columns standing on the Piazzetta di San Marco from the Orient. Immediately after the Pescheria, again on the right bank, extends the impressive façade of the **Fabbriche Nuove di Rialto**. The building was put up in 1552 by Jacopo Sansovino and occupied by public offices having to do with trade and commerce. The effect of the whole, a 25-arch-long portico with two upper floors of neo-Classical gabled windows, is, in truth, a bit monotonous.

The Fabbriche Nuove di Rialto.

A bit beyond the Fabbriche Nuove we are struck by the colorful bustle of the openair fruit and vegetable market. The building bordering the market-place, known as the **Fabbriche Vecchie di Rialto** was erected by Scarpagnino in 1522 as the seat of the court house.

Facing the two Fabbriche is the **Ca' Da Mosto.** One of the most picturesque in Venice, this Venetian Byzantine-style palace was built in the 13th century and was the home of the Da Mosto family, the celebrated Venetian navigators.

The Fabbriche Nuove di Rialto.

The Fabbriche Vecchie di Rialto.

The Fondaco dei Tedeschi.

The Grand Canal now curves right and we are left speechless by the sight which meets our eyes upon passing the curve: before us is the **Ponte di Rialto**, or **Rialto Bridge**, in all its splendor. (We shall soon discuss it in greater detail.)

First, let us stop an instant and take a look at the **Fondaco dei Tedeschi** (German Storehouse) to our left. The building we see today was built in 1515 over the site of a pre-existing structure destroyed in a fire. It was designed by Scarpagnino in the Renaissance style with a spacious round-arch portico on the ground floor and a border of white crenellation on top. Unfortunately, nothing remains of the frescoes by Giorgione and Titian that originally adorned the façade. Now a post office, the building once served as the official headquarters for the German merchants in Venice.

To the right is the **Palazzo dei Camerlenghi**, which was originally the Treasury of the Republic of St. Mark and thus the city's financial center. The ground floor was fitted with prison cells for those caught cheating on taxes. The building was erected in the early 16th century by Guglielmo Bergamasco. Two types of windows were employed: plain rectangular ones on the lower floor and rounded arch windows on the upper ones. Each storey is set off by a cornice decorated with a delicate frieze. And thus we have reached the bridge which is one of the most famous, if not the most famous, in the whole world, the Ponte di Rialto.

THE RIALTO BRIDGE

This is one of the best places to view the Grand Canal in all its charm. The Rialto is the oldest of the three bridges spanning the canal. Originally made of wood, it caved in 1440 and was rebuilt, again of wood, but this time with the addition of several shops along it. It had a special mechanism which allowed the middle section to be moved, whereby even the tallest masted ships could sail through. It was somewhat unstable, though, and thus in the 16th century it was decided to build a new bridge. A competition was called, drawing the participation of such wellknown architects as Michelangelo, Palladio, and Sansovino, all of whom worked on the project for years. Antonio Da Ponte, a relative unknown in such illustrious company, was awarded the commission and designed the bridge which was not finished until 1592. The Rialto is a single span bridge whose span measures 90 feet (the narrowest crossing of the Grand Canal is here) and has a maximum height of 24 feet at the middle. The two ends rest upon 12,000 pylons sunk into the muddy depths. The twenty-four shops lining the bridge are separated by a double arcade from which you can walk out on the terraces and get a superb view along the Grand Canal.

Aerial view of the Rialto Bridge. On the next two pages: *the Rialto Bridge seen from the Grand Canal.*

Palazzo Grimani; below:
Palazzo Loredan and
Palazzo Farsetti.

Palazzo Pisani-Moretta; right: *Palazzo Papadopoli.*

Just beyond the Rialto Bridge, on the right, is the **Palazzo dei Dieci Savi,** an early 16th century Renaissance building designed by Scarpagnino. Farther ahead on the left bank are the 13th century **Palazzo Loredan** and the 12th century **Palazzo Farsetti** (today the Venice City Hall), typical examples of the Venetian Byzantine style. The lower floors, are characterized by graceful elongated arches running the length of the ground and second floors.

The upper floors and balconies date from a 16th century alteration. On the same side, just a bit ahead, is a remarkable 16th century Renaissance building, Sanmicheli's masterpiece the **Palazzo Grimani.** Today, the three storey palace with its handsome arcading, is occupied by the Venice Court of Appeals. On the right bank is the **Palazzo Papadopoli,** a 16th century building designed by Giacomo dei Grigi in the Classical style.

The Ca' Foscari.

Palazzo Rezzonico;
below: *Palazzo Bernardo.*

Next comes a fine 15th century Gothic palace, **Palazzo Bernardo**, in which the Duke of Milan, Francesco Sforza. resided for some time. Past the **Rio San Polo** on the right bank, is an impressive 15th century building, the **Palazzo Pisani** with an intricate decorative motif adorning the center windows. Proceeding on the right, is the **Palazzo Balbi,** also known as "Palazzo in volta de Canal" (Corner Palace, because of its corner location). Here the Grand Canal swings leftward and, on the right, by the Rio Ca' Foscari, is a famous 15th century Gothic building, the **Ca' Foscari.**

Commissioned by Doge Francesco Foscari who ruled the Republic for over thirty years, it is now the Economics and Business School of the University of Venice. In 1574 Henry III of France was a guest in Ca' Foscari. During his week's sojourn, the city welcomed him with great pomp and put on an endless parade of festivities in his honor.

The façade of Ca' Foscari has been acclaimed as one of the finest and best-proportioned in all of Venice. On the ground floor, six plain arched windows flank the great portal, while the upper floors are adorned with beautiful carved loggias whose lacy designs become more intricate with each storey.

A bit farther along the left bank rises the 18th century **Palazzo Grassi,** built in 1718 by Giorgio Massari for the Grassi family of Bologna, and now occupied by the **Costume Institute**. The Classical façade has a rusticated stone ground floor and plain windows set off by simple balconies running the length of the two upper floors.

Opposite Palazzo Grassi on the right bank is a beautiful example of Venetian Classical architecture, the **Palazzo Rezzonico**. The ground and second floors were designed by Baldassarre Longhena who actually started construction in 1660 on a commission from the Priuli-Bon family. The building then came into the ownership of the Rezzonico family, who commissioned Giorgio Massari, the same architect who worked on Palazzo Grassi to finish it, although it was not fully completed until 1747. The façade has a rusticated stone ground floor, while the two upper stories are adorned with balconies and columns which set off the individual windows. Inside the palace is the **Museum of 18th Century Venice.**

Palazzo Grassi.

Top left: **Palazzo Barbaro**; center: **The Accademia Bridge**; bottom: **Palazzo Venier dei Leoni,** *home of the Guggenheim Collection of Modern Art.*

A bit farther on to the right is the 15th century Gothic **Palazzo Loredan dell'Ambasciatore** with its handsome façade. Inside the niches on either side are 15th century Lombard sculptures. Facing Palazzo Loredan is another 15th century Gothic building, **Palazzo Falier**, characterized by loggias on either side. We have now reached the last of the three bridges spanning the Grand Canal, the **Ponte dell'Accademia.** This bridge too has only a single span. Although it appears to be completely made of wood, its weight-bearing members are, for safety's sake, actually metal. Before 1930, a 19th century all metal bridge stood in its place, but it was torn down because it clashed too much with the rest of the Grand Canal's harmonious style.

Beyond the bridge on the left is a turn-of-the-19th century building, the **Palazzo Cavalli-Franchetti** whose façade was inspired by the Venetian Gothic style. On the opposite bank is another fine Gothic building, the **Palazzo Da Mula** which dates from the end of the 15th century.

Palazzo Cavalli-Franchetti.

Palazzo Corner, known as *Ca'Grande*.

The church of Santa Maria della Salute.

Farther on, on the same side, is a palace set in a lovely green park, the **Palazzo Venier dei Leoni** which houses Peggy Guggenheim's fabulous collection of modern art.

Facing it is the attractive **Casina delle Rose** (Rose House) in which two celebrated Italians, Canova, the 18th century sculptor, and D'Annunzio, the early 20th century writer, lived at various times. On the left is the headquarters of the local prefecture, **Palazzo Corner**, also known as **Ca' Granda** (Big House) whose impressive size undoubtedly brought about its nickname. Jacopo Corner commissioned the architect Jacopo Sansovino to build it in 1535. Three centuries later, it was occupied by the Austrian governor. Opposite the Ca' Granda is the **Palazzo Dario**, a Renaissance building erected by Pietro Lombardo in 1487, whose façade is adorned with multicolor decorative motifs and marble ornamentation.

Proceeding on the left is the 15th century Venetian Gothic **Palazzo Contarini-Fasan**, which has been dubbed "Desdemona's House". On the right we are struck by the sight of the majestic **church of Santa Maria della Salute** looming before us. This magnificent building is the masterpiece of Baldassarre Longhena, whose contribution to the appearance of the Grand Canal was considerable.

Aerial view of the Punta della Dogana.

Beyond the church is the **Punta della Dogana** upon which stands a 17th century tower surmounted by a globe supposed to mean good luck. From the 15th century onwards, duty on goods arriving from overseas was exacted on this spot.

We are now at the place where the Grand Canal empties into the huge stretch of waterfront by St. Mark's. As soon as we get off our vaporetto at the **Pontile di San Marco**, we are standing before a Lombard-style building erected in the 15th century. In the past it was occupied first by the Magistrato della Farina (Flour Magistrate) then by the Academy of Painters and Sculptors (from 1756 to 1807, when it was headed by G. B. Tiepolo), and presently it is the headquarters of the Venice Port Authority. Inside is a hall with a ceiling fresco by Jacopo Guarana (1773) depicting the *Triumph of Art*. Proceeding, we soon arrive at the **Giardinetto del Palazzo Reale.**

The park is on the site of the building which served as a storehouse for wheat. At the end of the garden we see the imposing **Palazzo della Zecca** designed by Sansovino in 1535. The rusticated stone arcading, Doric on the first and Ionic on the second floor, conveys an effect of stateliness and power, quite fitting for the Mint of the Republic of St. Mark. Here, in fact the Venetians minted their celebrated Zecchini d'oro (gold coins), the counterpart of the equally-renowned gold florins of Florence, both of which were widely circulated throughout Europe and even in the Orient. In 1870 the Zecca was closed down and since 1905 the reading room of the Marciana Library has occupied the building.

SECOND ITINERARY

ST. MARK'S SQUARE

S an Marco is the Venetians' incredible open-air drawing room, unique in all the world. Throughout its long, long history it has been witness to an endless stream of human events involving people from every walk of life, from the humblest artisans to the highest-ranking authorities, all of whom had a hand in creating the precious, incomparable treasure that is Venice. Looking back on the square's origins, we shall leave the description to a long-ago chronicler, Giuseppe Tassini, whose knowledge of his native town was truly incredible. In his book entitled Curiosità Veneziane (Venetian Curiosities), he recounts, "In olden times the Piazza San Marco was truly rustic. It was dubbed « morso » (tough) perhaps because its terrain was harder and tougher than the surrounding area and « brolo » (garden) because it was grassy and bordered by trees. On the opposite banks of the Batario Canal which crossed it were the two little churches of San Teodoro and San Gemignano erected, as is well-known, by Narsete who vanquished the Goths with the aid of the Venetian navy".

Preceding page: ***aerial view of St. Mark's Square***

Aerial view of St. Mark's Square and the Doges' Palace.

At the time the St. Mark's Basilica and the Doges' Palace were being built and then, during the reign of Doge Sebastiano Ziani (1172-1178), the Batario was filled in and the lawn in front of the building ripped out so the huge space could be paved to practically where it extends today. On either side, elegant houses with arcades running their length were erected. A number of them were taken over by the Procuratori di San Marco (magistrates) from whom their present name Procuratie derives. In 1264 the square was repaved in bricks forming a herringbone pattern which was left untouched until 1723 when a more modern design of grey trachyte from the Euganean and white marble, created by Andrea Tirali, was laid in its place. Today the square is a trapezoid measuring 569 feet in length, 266 feet on the church side, and 185 feet on the opposite side. At dusk when the lights go on, St. Mark's becomes especially enchanting: the arcades and open space come alive with music from the outdoor cafes while Venetians and out-of-towners leisurely stroll about or just sit enjoying the passing parade.

The façade of St. Mark's Basilica; below: *the copies of the famous bronze horses on the basilica terrace.*

THE CLOCKTOWER

The great clock, by *Giampaolo* and *Giancarlo Ranieri* (late XV century).

Facing the church, the Clocktower is on your left. It was built by Mauro Coducci between 1496 and 1499. The wings were added during 1500-1506, supposedly after a design by Pietro Lombardo, and later raised by Giorgio Massari in 1755. Above the tower is an open terrace on which stands a bell with a figure on either side. The bell is sounded by the hammering of the two male figures that were cast in bronze by Ambrogio de la Anchore in 1496 and dubbed the Moors because of the dark coloring they have taken on as their metallic surfaces have weathered over the almost five hundred years they have been striking the hours in Venice.

Right: *the Winged Lion, symbol of Venice;* below: *the two Moors atop the tower.*

Beneath the terrace, is the *winged lion,* symbol of *St. Mark the Evangelist* and the *city of Venice* herself. Below the lion is a jutting semi-circular balcony with a niche in the middle and a door on either side. The niche contains a gilded copper statue of the *Virgin and Child* which has been attributed to the sculptor and goldsmith Alessandro Leopardi who was born sometime in the second half of the 15th century and died 1522-1523. Each year on the feast-day of the Ascension (which comes 40 days after Easter) and during the whole time of Ascension week festivities, at the striking of every hour,

The clocktower.

figures of the Three Magi preceded by an angel, go in and out the doors, pass in front of the Virgin, and bow before her. This charming tradition is still observed and is truly one of the most picturesque sights to be enjoyed during springtime in Venice. Below the semi-circular balcony is the huge face of the intricate clock works placed there at the end of the 15th century. It was created by two craftsmen, father and son, Giampaolo and Giancarlo Ranieri from Parma. The clock also indicates the changing of the seasons, the movement of the sun, the hours, and the phases of the moon. It was restored in 1757 by Bartolomeo Ferracina.

The Procuratie Vecchie and the Napoleonic Wing, home of the Correr Museum.

THE PROCURATIE VECCHIE - NAPOLEONIC WING - THE PROCURATIE NUOVE

Extending the length of the Clocktower side of the square is the building known as the **Procuratie Vecchie** which has fifty arches on the ground floor level and two upper floors of loggias. It was begun between the end of the 15th and first half of the 16th centuries by Mauro Coducci who designed the first floor. Following the fire of 1512, Bartolomeo and Guglielmo Grigi succeeded Coducci and added the second storey, although the building was completed by Sansovino. The name "Procuratie Vecchie" (Old Magistrature) was given to distinguish the building from the "Procuratie Nuove" (New Magistrature) whose design is in keeping with the earlier building, so that the square conveys an effect of stately harmony and balance. On the far side of the square, the site of San Gemignano, a very old church which Napoleon ordered torn down in 1807 so that a huge ballroom entered from the royal palace, Palazzo Reale, could go up in its place, is the **Ala Nuovissima** (Brand-new Wing) or the **Ala Napoleonica** (Napoleonic Wing)). It is a neo-Classical design by Giuseppe Soli, who repeated the double orders of the Procuratie Nuove, adding a frieze of statues of Roman emperors and mythological and allegorical scenes to the top level. On the south side of the square is the **Procuratie Nuove**. Influenced by the Classical style of Sansovino's Library, Vincenzo Scamozzi designed it in 1584 and supervised construction up to the tenth arch. The rest was continued by Baldassarre Longhena, who finished it in 1640. This building too was once the residence of the Procuratori di San Marco but when the Republic fell in 1797 it was turned into the royal palace. Today it is occupied by cultural institutes such as the Correr and Archeological Museums.

THE BELLTOWER

This is the oldest belltower in Venice, having been built over Roman foundations, starting from the time of Doge Pietro Tribuno (888-912) and then off and on over the years. Among the numerous artists who had a hand in it were Niccolo Barattieri and Bartolomeo Malfatto (the bell chamber), Proto Bon and Giorgio Spavento. For centuries it withstood the onslaught of storms and earthquakes. Then, at 10 a.m. on July 14, 1902, weakened by centuries of vicissitudes and less than perfect workmanship, it suddenly collapsed, luckily without causing a single victim or damage to the nearby monuments (except for Sansovino's Loggetta which was shattered into fragments and buried beneath the rubble). The loggia was put back piece by piece and the belltower itself was reconstructed exactly as it had been on the same spot. It was re-opened to the public on the feast-day of St. Mark, the patron saint of the city, in 1912. All of Venice joined in the celebrations to welcome back the "*paron de casa*" (master of the house) as the Venetians dubbed the building whose bell chamber commands a remarkable view over the whole city and the lagoon. A convenient elevator will take you up to the bell chamber of the 320-foot tower. On top of the cusp is a gilded angel weathervane. When the tower collapsed in 1902, four of its five bells, the Angel, and the nearby Loggetta were all smashed to pieces, but they were put back together again with the painstaking labor of a Venetian craftsman, Emanuele Munaretti. Each of the five bells has a particular nickname

The belltower.

Piazzetta di San Marco.

and a specific purpose: "*La Marangona*" (carpenter) which was sounded as a signal for the laborers employed on the Arsenal project to start and stop work; "*La Nona*" which was rung at noon; "*La Trottiera*" which was rung when the aristocrats rode to the Senate at the time the city was still only partly paved; "*La Pregadi*" which announced meetings of the Greater Council (whose members were known as pregadi); "*La Pinghiera*" or "*La Maleficio*", also known as the Justice Bell, because it tolled half an hour before public executions. Also jutting from the square side was a cage inside of which criminals were exposed day and night until the practice was abolished towards the middle of the 16th century. Another, less depressing, tradition was linked to the belltower. The spectacle, known as the "*Flight of the Angel*" took place the last Thursday before Carnival. A rope was stretched between the bell chamber and the loggia of the Doges' Palace and an acrobat with a safety cord around his waist would walk across to the Palace where the Doge was waiting with a bouquet of flowers for him. Emperors kings, cardinals, ambassadors, all made the climb up the Belltower, but undoubtedly its most famous guest was Galileo Galilei who climbed it for the purpose of demonstrating his newly-invented telescope to the Venetian VIPs.

THE LOGGETTA

At the foot of the Belltower is the marvelous three-arched loggetta built by Sansovino between 1537 and 1549 to replace a 13th century one which, moved from the neighborhood of San Basso, had been erected here. In 1569 it housed the Armed Guard of the Republic when the Greater Council was in session. The four bronze statues in the niches of the facade depict *Apollo, Mercury, Pax* (Peace) and *Minerva* each symbolizing an aspect of the Republic: Apollo, its power; Mercury, the eloquence of its ambassadors and intellectuals; Peace, supposed to inspire the Venetians' political activities; and Minerva, the high-level attained in the arts, sciences, government and war. The four statues are proof of the great skill that their creator, Sansovino himself, had achieved as sculptor in his mature period. The fine bronze gateway and putti on either side of the top are by Antonio Gai (1735). The allegorical reliefs (alluding to Venetian power) have been ascribed to Tiziano Minio and Danese Cattaneo. Facing the church are three tall bronze flag-poles which once flew the colors of the Republic. Remarkable works of art, they were crafted in 1505 by a sculptor-goldsmith, Alessandro Leopardi. The center one is especially noteworthy for the expressive profile of Doge Leonardo Loredan inscribed in a medallion.

The Loggetta Sansoviniana.

The cathedral of Venice went up along with the Republic's rise as a sea power. In the year 828 the mortal remains of St. Mark the Evangelist were triumphantly borne to Venice and safety, far from the desecration supposedly in store from the Moslems of Alexandria of Egypt. Welcomed with solemn ceremonies and rites, the relics were at first placed in the Palatium Chapel, actually the tiny Church of San Teodoro. But it was hardly worthy of the new - and now sole - patron saint of the *Serenissima Repubblica*, so Doge Giustiniano Partecipazio decided to remedy the situation by bequeathing a considerable sum of money for the building of a basilica befitting such valuable relics. His wish was carried out by his brother, Giovanni Partecipazio, who set about the huge task of erecting a church alongside the Doges' Palace in 829. By 832 the building had all its main structures up and by 883 it was fully decorated.

St. Mark's Basilica, detail of the center door.

Center door to the Basilica, with the Last Judgement, by *L. Querena.*

In 976, during an uprising of the Venetians against the espotic doge, Pietro Candiano IV, the Doges' Palace was set on fire and the flames also damaged the adjoining basilica, which was only restored years later by the canonized doge, Pietro Orseolo. Then, shortly after the year 1000, Doge Domenico Contarini decided that the basilica was not equal to the magnificent churches being built in all the mainland cities and had it demolished. In its place he commissioned the church as we know it today.

According to a number of reliable scholars, the grandiose project got underway in 1063, whereas others maintain that it was begun several years later and never finished under Contarini's dogeship. The plan picked by the doge was wholly Byzantine, a Greek cross shape covered by a series of domes (although the treatment was more Romanesque than Byzantine), yet the name of the architect has not come down to us. In any case, the building was finished in 1073. Originally rather plain, if not austere-looking, St. Mark's was soon adorned with superb mosaics, precious marble from Roman Altinum, and various architectural and decorative elements from the Orient.

For centuries, Venetian travelers, merchants, and admirals carted off war spoils and souvenirs to donate to the great church, so that today St. Mark's is a complex yet harmonious combination of Byzantine, Gothic, Islamic and Renaissance elements.

The Tetrarchs.

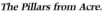

The Pillars from Acre.

THE FAÇADE

Along its approximately 169 feet runs a porch of five rounded arches protruding into the square. A delicate marble railing separates the ground floor level from the upper one with the four famous gilded bronze horses. The whole building, dominated by five Oriental domes, seems unreal, almost as if it were a stage set. Before taking a more detailed look at the façade, we shall stop to observe the south side of the façade (i.e., that closest to the Doges' Palace). On the corner is a porphyry sculptural group showing two pairs of embracing male figures. The famous sculpture called "*the Tetrarchs*" is thought to be Syrian and most likely represents four emperors, namely Diocletian, Massimian, Galerius, and Constans. Nearby are two square columns which were brought here from St. John d'Acre in Syria. On the upper section of the church is a Byzantine mosaic depicting the *Virgin*. One of the perpetually-lit lamps near it recalls the legend of the poor baker's boy unjustly executed for a crime he never committed.

On the corner bordering the square is a

truncated column, the "*pietra del bando*" (decree stone), which came from Syria. Here all the laws passed by the government were read aloud to the people assembled below.

The Translation of St. Mark's Body to the Basilica.

We shall now take a closer look at the five portals opening into the square (starting from the right). In the first one bearing elaborate Moorish decorative motifs is a mosaic showing the *Removal of St. Mark's Body from Alexandria in Egypt,* a 17th century work by Pietro Vecchia. In the second one is another mosaic by Vecchia of the *Arrival of St. Mark's Body in Venice.* The central one is adorned with fine Venetian Romanesque bas-reliefs depicting *Professions, Months* and *Virtues.* Above the portal is a fine 12th century Romanesque sculpture of the *Angel Appearing to St. Mark.* The mosaic above, representing the *Last Judgement* is a 19th century work after a design by Lattanzio Querena.

The Venetians Venerating the Body of St. Mark.

The Arrival of St. Mark's Body in Venice.

 The fourth portal has a bronze door cast in the 14th century by Master Bertuccio. Above is a mosaic of the *Body of St. Mark Being Venerated by the Venetians,* by Sebastiano Ricci (1728). The fifth portal is called the **Portal of Sant'Alipio** after the statue of the saint to be found here. It is adorned with columns, capitals, and reliefs of various origins, mainly Byzantine, removed from older church buildings. The mosaic, datable 1260-1270, and showing the *Venetians Carrying the Body of St. Mark into the Church* is especially fascinating because it allows us to see what St. Mark's looked like at the time.

The Removal of St. Mark's Body from Alexandria.

If you want a closer look at the works on the upper floor of the façade, you are allowed to walk out on the terrace from the galleries inside the church. However, to get a proper overall view of the façade, we recommend taking time out to walk far back on the square to embrace the whole with a single glance. Beneath the elegant marble terracing between the arches are noteworthy 12th century Byzantine reliefs. From left to right, they portray: *Hercules and the Wild Boar, the Virgin, St. George, St. Demetrius, the Archangel Gabriel* and *Hercules and the She-Deer.* On the loggia above the main portal are the four marvelous 4th century B.C. *Greek horses* that Enrico Dandolo brought to Venice from Constantinople in 1204. They were on this spot from about 1250 until 1798 when Napoleon carted them off to Paris (they were returned to Venice in 1815). The horses were removed twice for safekeeping during both world wars. Behind the horses are four 11th century eight-sided columns with fine carved capitals and the huge window of the central arch. The mosaics in the smaller arches on either side, based on cartoons by Maffeo da Verona, portray (from left to right): the *Deposition*, the *Descent into Limbo*, the *Resurrection,* and the *Ascension.* The elaborate decoration of the upper floor is one of the most remarkable sculptural compositions to have come out of Italian Gothic. Art historians believe that the project was begun by the Dalle Masegne family in 1385. Then, after a great fire in 1419 it was restored, continued, and altered by various Florentine and Lombard artists.

The Deposition from the Cross.

Descent into Limbo.

Resurrection.

Ascension.

LEFT SIDE OF ST. MARK'S, THE PIAZZETTA DEI LEONCINI,
and THE PORTA DEI FIORI

On the north side of the church is the Piazzetta dei Leoncini (literally, Square of the Lions) named after the two marble lions sculpted by Giovanni Bonazza in 1722. Before the Porta dei Fiori (Flower Portal) are three arches surmounted by fine Gothic sculptures. In the center of the first arch is a symbolic representation of the 12 Apostles (12 lambs). Then, after a relief of *Alexander the Great Carried up to Heaven,* a 10th century work, between the first and second arches, we find ourselves before the Porta dei Fiori. Unfortunately, nothing remains of the original construction, probably datable around 1200, the period when this side of the church was being remodeled. The Arab-Moorish style arch which has elaborate carvings of flowers and branches (and a lunette relief of a *Nativity*) gave the portal its name. After the fourth arch are five 12th and 13th century Byzantine reliefs in the protrubances, the finest of which shows *Christ Blessing the Four Evangelists.* Farther on, beneath an arch, is the *tomb of Daniele Manin* by Luigi Borro. Manin died in Paris in 1857 and his remains were brought to his native city in 1868. Facing the Piazzetta is the Baroque façade of the suppressed **church of San Basso**, attributed to Giuseppe Benoni, and built c. 1670. In the center are marble fountains in the form of well-curbs and on the far side is the **Palazzo Patriarcale** with a neo-Classical façade by Lorenzo Santi (1837-1850).

The Piazzetta dei Leoncini.

The atrium of the Basilica.

THE ATRIUM OF ST. MARK'S

In order to get the best possible view of the atrium, enter through the main portal. All aglow with a splendid mantle of golden mosaic, the atrium space is divided, by slightly pointed arches, into separate bays closed off by hemispherical domes, except for the central one (by the portal through which we entered) which is open. Measuring 201 x 19 feet and almost 24 feet tall, the atrium has remained unchanged for seven hundred years. The pavement too is covered with mosaics that create incredible light effects when the church is flooded, as it often is, in fall and winter. The marble columns against the walls are of various origins, some are even said to have come from the Temple of Solomon in Jerusalem.

Following the numbers on the map is the best way to look at the porch mosaics which recount stories from the Old and New Testaments.

Practically all the mosaics were executed by Venetian masters who demonstrated incredible technical skill in their treatment of color and form. Their lively narrative style is typical of the Romanesque period.

7 - The Porta di San Giovanni is opposite the Porta dei Fiori. On the dome and lunette are *Scenes from the Life of Moses* and, in the spandrels, figures of *Solomon, David, Zechariah,* and *Malachi*. Directly over the door is the *Virgin and Child Between Sts. John and Mark.*

8 - The dome recess contains 17th century mosaics executed after designs by Pietro Vecchio showing *Sts. Apollinaire, Sigismund* and *St. Francis with the Stigmata. Scenes from the Life of Joseph* (13th century) cover the dome, with the four *Evangelists* in the spandrels.

9 - The *Scenes from the Life of Joseph* are continued. The tomb in the exedra is that of Doge Marino Morosini who died in 1253.

10 - The mosaic in the semi-dome, executed in 1583 by Giuseppe Bianchini after a cartoon by Salviati, shows the *Judgment of Solomon*. The dome has *Scenes from the Life of Joseph,* with four *Hebrew Prophets* in the spandrels. All of these mosaics were done in 1240, but they underwent extensive restoration in the 19th century. An anonymous Pisan sculptor carved the *tomb of Doge Bartolomeo Gradenigo,* who died in 1342, which is visible in the exedra.

11 - The lunette of the **Porta di San Pietro** has a Byzantine mosaic of *St. Peter*. The dome and side lunette contain several *Scenes from the Life of Abraham* in the Romanesque-Byzantine style.

12 - The 13th century ceiling mosaic shows the *Drunkenness* and *Death of Noah,* the *Construction of the Tower of Babel,* and the *Weeping and Wailing of the Multitude*. The sepulchral wall contains the *tomb of Felicita Michiel,* wife of Doge Vitale Falier, who died in 1101.

Preceding page: **the atrium of the Basilica.**
Below: **the vault of the atrium,** *a splendid gallery glowing with mosaics.*

13 - In the upper niches is a *Virgin With Saints;* in the lower ones, *Apostles.* These works were done in the 12th century and were influenced by the Ravennate school. The bronze panel on the portal has figures of saints cast between 1112 and 1138. The mosaic in the semi-dome, by Valerio and Francesco Zuccato who executed it in 1545 after a design by Titian, depicts *St. Mark in Ecstasy.* The same craftsmen also carried out the ceiling decoration (after designs by Pordenone) in 1549. The mosaics represent the *Resurrection of Lazarus,* the *Crucifixion,* the *Deposition,* and the *Death of the Virgin,* with *Evangelists* and *Prophets* in the spandrels. The red marble slab on the pavement marks the exact spot where the Emperor Frederick Barbarossa fell to his knees before Pope Alexander III on July 23, 1177.

Above: **Scenes from the Story of Noah and the Flood;** right: **Scenes from the Life of Moses** (*detail of the mosaics in the atrium*).
Opposite page: **The Creation of the World.**

14 - Fifteen marvelous *Scenes from the Life of Noah* and the *Flood* decorate the inside of the archway. On the outside is the niche *tomb of Doge Vitale Falier* who died in 1096.

15 - The bronze panels of the **Porta San Clemente** are divided into 28 rectangular sections, each bearing a figure of a saint beneath which is a Greek inscription in silver (a Byzantine work executed in Constantinople). In the lunette is another mosaic by Valerio Zuccato of *St. Clement,* dated 1532. The three-part dome is decorated with mosaics dated c. 1230. They represent various *episodes of Genesis,* from the *Creation of Heaven and Earth* and the *Creation of Adam and Eve,* up to the *story of Cain and Abel.*

16 - The main entrance to the church. On the left is a door leading to the upper galleries and the museum.

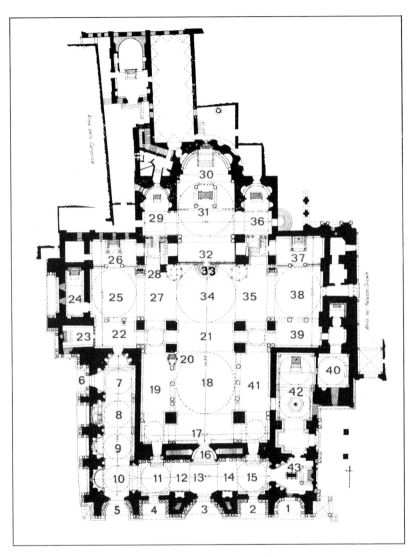

18. Dome of the Pentecost
19. Left nave
20. Capital of the Crucifix
21. West Arch
22. Door of the Virgin
23. Chapel of the Mascoli
24. Chapel of St. Isidore
25. Dome of St. John
26. Chapel of the Madonna Nicopeia
27. North Arch
28. Crypt of St. Mark
29. Chapel of St. Peter
30. Apse
31. Main Altar
32. East arch
33. Ambos
34. Dome of the Ascension
35. South Arch
36. Chapel of St. Clement
37. Altar of the Blessed Sacrament
38. Dome of St. Leonard
39. Right Transept
40. Treasure
41. Right nave
42. Baptistry
43. Zen chapel

What makes the interior of the church so striking is the unusual combination of simple architectural forms and an incomparable wealth of decorative motifs. The plan of the building, a Greek cross, has single aisles set off by round arches upon marble columns, mostly Byzantine in style, and gilded capitals. Five huge domes sustained by massive pillars crown the whole. The patterned flooring made of colored marble dates from the 12th century. Its unevenness is due to the shifting of the structure which rests on pylons. The church including the vestibule, is c. 249 feet long and c. 203 feet at the crossing; the center dome is c. 139 feet on the outside, and c. 91 on the inside.

An overall view of the interior of the Basilica.

The Doge supposedly told the unknown architect about to start work on the project that it should be the most beautiful building ever built. And so it was a vision of 4000 m² of glittery gilding and mosaics upon gold ground. The mosaic work was carried out by Venetian craftsmen in various campaigns. Noteworthy was the contribution of great Renaissance masters from Tuscany. The whole decorative scheme pivots around the theme of the glorification of the Church of the Savior. It would be practically impossible to describe all the mosaics, sculptures, and architectural elements in St. Mark's, so we shall proceed only with a description of the highlights. However, we recommend going to the upper galleries to best view the mosaics.

17 - Above the center portal is a 14th century mosaic of *Christ Blessing Between the Virgin and St. Mark*. In the arch above is a grandiose mosaic of the *Apocalypse According to St. John* by Pordenone and Zuccato (1570-1589). Behind the Apocalypse, against the center window, is the **Arcone del Paradiso** (Arch of Paradise) with *Scenes of the Last Judgement* executed in the 16th and 17th centuries. Major artists such as Jacopo Tintoretto, Antonio Vassillacchi, Maffeo da Verona, and Domenico Tintoretto contributed to the huge undertaking.

18 - The Pentecost Dome - In the center is the white dove symbolizing the *Holy Spirit* whose divine breath spreads out in the form of tongues of fire over the seated *Apostles*. Between the tiny arched windows are representations of the *Nations of Christendom* and, in the spandrels, monumental *Angels*. These mosaics date from the first half of the 12th century.

GRADUS ADEST HIC SERVANS HOSTIA PETRVS OVEM RESERAT DIGNIS OMNIBVS IPSE V

19 - Left aisle - The mosaics depict *Christ and Four Prophets* (13th century). Among the precious marbles adorning the wall are *Paradise* and the *Triumph of the Trinity* by G. Pilotti and the *Martyrdom of Apostles Peter and Paul* by Palma the Younger and Padovanino. The right arch contains the *Crucifixion of St. Andrew* by Aliense and the *Murder of St. Thomas* by Tizianello, the left one the *Miracles of St. John* by Patavino. These mosaics all date from the 17th century.

20 - The Capital of the Crucifix - This is a hexagonal shrine of six precious marble columns surmounted by carved Byzantine capitals. Inside is a panel painting showing a *Crucifixion* which probably came from Constantinople. According to a legend, it supposedly bled when a maniac attacked it with a knife.

21 - The Great Western Arch - The 12th century mosaic decoration has a dramatic rendition of *scenes of the Passion.* The episodes are shown in five

Paradise and *the Triumph of the Trinity,* mosaic by *G. Pilotti;* below: *the "Capital of the Crucifix", an hexagonal edicula with two XIV century statues portraying the Annunciation.*

*The Virgin with St. Mark and St. John the Evangelist, mable tryptych above the altar in the Mascoli Chapel, attributed to the Bon family; below: **the chapel of St. Isidore.***

separate compartments. The dramatic *Crucifixion* scenes are especially note-worthy.

22 - On the ceiling and wall are fine mosaics with *Scenes of the Life of the Virgin* and the childhood of *Christ*. The ceiling mosaics date from the 13th-14th centuries, those on the wall are 16th century works. Jacopo Tintoretto and Palma the Younger took part in the project.

23 - The Chapel of the Mascoli - Founded in 1430, it got its name in 1618 when it belonged to an all male religious confraternity. The sculptures have been ascribed to the Bon family. The fine mosaics, executed between 1430 and 1450, show *Scenes from the Life of the Virgin.* The two lefthand episodes are by Michele Giambono and the *Visitation* and the *Death of the Virgin* on the right were executed after cartoons by Jacopo Bellini and Andrea Mantegna.

24 - The Chapel of St. Isidore - The chapel was commissioned by Doge Andrea Dandolo between 1354 and 1355 to contain the mortal *remains of St. Isidore* which have been placed on the altar in a Venetian-Gothic sculpted urn. The 14th century mosaics cover-ing the walls and ceiling show fifteen *episodes from the life of St. Isidore* ren-dered in a lively narrative style.

25 - The Dome of St. John - It is adorned with 13th century mosaics in the Venetian-Gothic style showing Romanesque influence. The mosaics portray *Scenes from the Life of John* with four *saints* in the spandrels. Two of the saints, *Gregory* and *Jerome,* are by Giambattista Piazzetta.

The Chapel of the Madonna Nicopeia, the most venerated image in St. Mark's Basilica.

26 - The Chapel of the Madonna Nicopeia - Before entering the chapel, do not overlook the *Altar of St. Paul,* an exquisite Renaissance sculpture against the lefthand pillar. The carved altar frontal showing the *Conversion of St. Paul* has been attributed to Pietro Lombardo. The *statue of St. Paul* on the altar is in the style of Lombardo. The chapel contains the image of the *Madonna Nicopeia* (the Virgin Victorious) which is greatly venerated by the Venetians who consider her their protectress. The image, actually a Byzantine painting with Oriental enameling predating the year 1000, was brought to Venice from Constantinople by Doge Enrico Dandolo in 1204. The altar is by Tommaso Contino (1617), while the sculptures of the *Virgin and Saints* are 11th and 12th century Venetian-Gothic. The decorative mosaics beneath the arches were done over in the 17th century.

27 - The Great North Arch - The mosaics represent the *Wedding at Cana* and *Supper in the House of Simon* (after cartoons by Jacopo Tintoretto), *Christ Healing the Leper* by P.Veronese, and the *Healing of the Sick Man* and the *Resurrection of the Son of the Widow Naim* by Giuseppe Salviati. In the small arch are four *prophets*.

28 - The Crypt of St. Mark - The crypt beneath the choir, reached by a flight of stairs, has ribbed vaults upon Greek and Byzantine columns. The mortal *remains of St. Mark* were laid to rest here in 1094, but were later removed since the crypt, lying below the lagoon water level, was subject to periodic flooding. After extensive alteration, it was completely dried out and reopened to worship in 1889.

On this page: *two views of the old crypt, dating from the XI century.*

29 - The Chapel of St. Peter - Before the actual chapel is an "*iconostasis*" (rood screen) with five sculpted saints attributed to the school of the Dalle Masegne family. The relief of *St. Peter* on the smaller altar is a 14th century Venetian school work. The mosaics covering the walls portray *Scenes from the Lives of St. Mark and St. Peter* (2nd half of the 13th century). A door behind the altar of St. Peter leads to the **sacristy**, while the one on the left-hand side leads to the **church of San Teodoro.** The lovely Sacristy with its mosaic ceiling was built in 1486. The Christ in the center of the ceiling is probably by Titian, the four *Evangelists* around him and several figures of *Apostles* in the lunette of the righthand wall have been attributed to Lorenzo Lotto, and, in the recess of the portal, the figure of *God the Father* is by Padovanino. On either side of the portal are two figures of *St. Jerome,* pieces submitted to a competition held in 1563, by Domenico Bianchini known as "Il Rosso" (the Redhead) and his

The Chapel of St. Peter, on the altar, **St. Peter worshiped by two "procurators",** *bas-relief, XIV century.*

nephew, Giannantonio. The inlays on the three finely-executed cabinets portray *Scenes from the Life of St. Mark* still-lifes, and landscapes. Although crafted by several different artists, they seem to have an overall compositional pattern inspired by a single master whose style recalls Vittore Carpaccio's. In fact art historians believe that the extraordinary panels were based on Carpaccio cartoons. The **Chiesetta di San Teodoro**, now part of the sacristy, is in Renaissance style. In the past it was the headquarters of the Inquisition Court. Over the altar are sculptures by Sansovino and, on the wall, a mosaic of *St. John the Beggar* by Pietro Vecchia. To the left of the altar is the entrance to the **Aula Capitolare** (Chapter Room) containing a number of noteworthy paintings such as the *Adoration of the Shepherds* by G. B. Tiepolo and portraits of confraternity directors by followers of Gentile Bellini, Titian, B. Strozzi and Pietro Longhi.

St. Peter, *a mosaic in the vault of the apse in the chapel of St. Peter (XIII century).*

The Pala d'Oro, the golden altarpiece.

30 - The Apse - The apse is entered through the **Chapel of St. Peter.** The Byzantine mosaics between the windows, untouched by the fire of 1106, are the oldest in St. Mark's. They represent *Sts. Nicholas Peter, Mark,* and *Hermagora.* The door leading to the sacristy is by Sansovino.

31 - The Main Altar and Choir Dome - The main altar is surmounted by a tribune resting upon four precious columns made of Oriental albaster and covered with reliefs depicting *Scenes from the Lives of Christ and Mary* sculpted by 13th century Venetian masters. Above are statues of the *Savior* and the four *Evangelists.* To the left of the Ciborium are four bronze sculptures representing the *Evangelists* by

Sansovino and the four statues opposite them are the *Fathers of the Church* sculpted by Girolamo Pagliari in 1614. Inside the main altar are the *relics of the Evangelist Mark*, while over it is the celebrated masterpiece of Medieval gold-smithing the **Pala d'Oro**, by the Venetian master Giampaolo Boninsegna (1345). 10 feet long and almost 5 feet tall, it was originally commissioned from artists in Constantinople in 978, then embellished in 1105 with gold and enamels brought to Venice after the Fourth Crusade, of 1204 from the Monastery of the Pantocrator. Boninsegna is also responsible for the embossing and setting the gemstones. The Pala has eighty enamel plaques which illustrate *Scenes from the Lives of Christ,* the *Virgin,* and *St. Mark,* as well as figures of *angels, prophets,* the *Evangelists,* and *Oriental emperors.* The choir dome is covered with a mosaic of *Christ Pantocrator,* the *Virgin* and *Prophets,* with the figures of the *Evangelists* in the spandrels.

Christ Enthroned, Giving His Blessing,
detail of the mosaic on the vault of the
apse on the main altar.

Opposite page: **the main altar.**

32 - The Great Eastern Arch -
Opposite the main altar is an impressive rood screen. This consists of a colored marble railing on top of which eight columns support an architrave with statues of *St. Mark,* the *Virgin,* and the *Apostles.* The fourteen statues are by Jacobello and Pier Paolo Dalle Masegne (1394). The bronze and silver *Crucifix* in the center is by Jacopo and Marco Bennato. On either side of the choir are elaborate inlaid stalls crafted by a Jesuit, Fra Vincenzo, and four

lecterns decorated with bronzes by Sansovino. In the overhead arch are mosaics with *New Testament Scenes* from the *Life of Christ* executed after cartoons by Jacopo Tintoretto. The Doge and magistrates attended services here in the choir.

33 - On either side of the rood screen are two ambos (pulpits). On the left is the so-called **double ambo** dating from the 14th century: the lower one, for readings from the Epistles, is an eight-sided structure resting on eleven columns made of precious marble, while the upper one, for readings from the Gospel, rests upon seven columns and is covered with a gilded bronze dome. The ambo on the right is known as the **Pulpito della Reliquia** since on major feast-days relics of the saints were shown from it. Here the newly-elected Doge was presented to the people. The *statue of the Virgin* above has been attributed to Giovanni Bon.

34 -The Dome of the Ascension - It is decorated with a 13th century Byzantine mosaic in which western influence can be felt. The mosaic shows *Christ in Glory* surrounded by fluttering *angels* with the *Virgin* and *Apostles* assembled below. Between the windows are personifications of the sixteen *Virtues* that were essential characteristics of the living Christ. Figures of the *Evangelists* and the four sacred rivers mentioned in the Bible adorn the spandrels.

35 - The Great Southern Arch - The subjects of these superb 13th century mosaics are *Jesus Entering Jerusalem,* the *Temptation of Christ,* the *Last Supper,* and the *Washing of the Feet.* The *God the Father in Glory* in the center is a 17th century work by Giacomo Pasterini.

36 - The Chapel of St. Clement - This chapel, like the choir, is preceded by a red marble rood screen. Four columns support an architrave adorned with statues sculpted by the Dalle Masegnes in 1397. The relief on the altar depicting the *Virgin* is by Pirgotele (1465). The Doge could hear Mass without being seen by listening at the barred window to the right of the altar. On the left is a *reliquary* also sculpted by the Dalle Masegnes. The scenes illustrated in the ceiling are the *Removal of the Body of St. Mark from Alexandria,* the *Departure from Egypt,* and the *Arrival in Venice.* The mosaics beyond the organ with *Scenes from the Life of St. Clement* date from the 13th century.

The chapel of St. Clement.

37 - The Altar of the Blessed Sacrament - In front of the altar is a pair of bronze candlesticks by Maffeo Olivieri (1527). On the right is a 15th century relief depicting *St. Peter* amidst the worshippers and, on the left, a Byzantine *Virgin*. Against a column is an *Angel* in front of which burns an *eternal light* in memory of the prodigious discovery of the body of St. Mark. The mosaics in the arch depict the *Parables* and *Miracles of Christ,* whereas those covering the wall above the altar and between the windows illustrate *Scenes from the Life of St. Leonard* to whom the altar had originally been dedicated. Pietro Vecchia is the author of the mosaics.

38 - The Dome of St. Leonard - These 13th century mosaics contain images of several saints greatly venerated by the Venetians: *Sts. Leonard, Nicholas, Biagio* and *Tecla* by Vincenzo Bastiani (1512). Under the small inner arch are other 15th mosaics with figures of *saints*. On the outer one

Some of the precious objects in the treasury of St. Mark's Basilica.

around the Gothic rose-window dating from the 15th century are fine mosaics narrating the *Miracles of Christ* by G. Pauletti. The Doge entered the church through the door beneath the rose-window.

39 - The Right Transept - At the far side is the entrance to the Treasury. Over the door is a 13th century *Moorish arch*. In a lunette between two mosaic angels is a 14th century *Ecce Homo*. Underneath the lefthand arches are mosaic renderings of *Sts. Geminiano* and *Saverio*.

40 - The Treasury of St. Mark - Preceding the treasury is the so-called "*Sanctuary*" which has a collection of 110 reliquaries as well as other sacred pieces. The Treasury contains the relics and precious artifacts that the Venetians acquired through trade or as war booty over the centuries.

41 - The Righthand Aisle - The right wall is covered with superb Venetian school mosaics showing both Byzantine and Romanesque influence. They represent the *Virgin in Prayer and Four Prophets* (1230). Beneath the last arch is a huge *holy water font* composed of a basin carved out of a single piece of porphyry and decorated with sculptures by the Lombardos.

42 - The Baptistry - The Venetians call it "*Chiesa dei Putti*" (Church of the Putti), since infants are baptized here. Doge Andrea Dandolo (who is buried here) commissioned it in 1350. The huge *baptismal font* was designed by Jacopo Sansovino and beautifully crafted by Desiderio Fiorentino, Tiziano Minio, and Francesco Segala. The bronze lid is decorated with figures of *Evangelists* and *Scenes from the Life of St. John the Baptist.* The *statuette of St. John the Baptist* is also by Segala (1575). Before the altar is the tomb of one of the Venetian greats, Jacopo Sansovino, a gilded silver altar front embossed with figures of *saints* and 13th and 14th century Byzantine reliefs protraying the *Baptism of Christ* and *Sts. George and Theodore.* Here too the ceilings, lunettes, and domes are adorned with 14th century mosaics. The finest of these are *Christ and the Apostles Preaching the Gospel* and the *Herod's Banquet* (on the dome), *Christ in Glory Amidst the Heavenly Hosts* (on the dome above the altar) and *Scenes from the Life of St. John the Baptist* and the *Crucifixion* (on the lunettes and walls).

43 - The Zen Chapel - The Republic decreed the erection of this superb chapel in memory of Cardinal G. Battista Zen who, before he died in 1501, bequeathed a rich legacy to his native city. The *cardinal's tomb* in the center was cast in bronze by Paolo

Savin. The other sculptures and bronzes are by Savin and others (Pietro Campanato, A. Leonardi, and A. Lombardo). On the bronze altar is a statue, also in bronze, known as the "*Virgin of the Shoe*", since, according to a legend, a shoe donated to the image by a poor man miraculously turned into solid gold. The 14th century mosaics recount the *Life of St Mark.* In the apse semi-dome is the *Virgin and Child with Angels* while on the wall is a Byzantine relief, with a Greek inscription, of another *Virgin.* In Lombard-style niches are lovely *statuettes of four prophets*, a superb Venetian-Romanesque *Nativity* and, on either side of the altar, a pair of marble *lions.*

Retracing our steps, we return to the atrium where we climb the stairs to the **MARCIANO MUSEUM** which has a superb collection of tapestries, rugs, old lace, and other works of art. The highlights are: the *organ panels* by Gentile Bellini, ten tapestries with *Scenes from the Passion of Christ* (after designs by Zannino di Pietro), four tapestries with *Stories from the Life of St. Mark* (executed in 1551 after designs by Sansovino) and an *altarpiece* by Paolo Veneziano dated 1345. One of Veneziano's masterpieces, the altarpiece once served as the cover for the Pala d'Oro in the main altar and has *Scenes from the Life of St Mark*, the *Dead Christ* and the *Virgin and Saints.*

Opposite page: *view of the XIV mosaics on the vaults and lunettes in the Baptistry*; in the foreground, *the statue of St. John the Baptist* by *Francesco Segala.*

The Museo Civico Correr occupies the so-called Napoleonic or "Nuovissima" wing (west side) and the Procuratie Nuove (south side). The entrance is from the arcade of the Napoleonic wing. The collection was begun in 1830 by a wealthy Venetian nobleman, Teodoro Correr, who bequeathed his fabulous art works to his native city. The museum remained in the Palazzo Correr on the Grand Canal until 1922 when it was moved to its present site. The collection was so big it had to be split up into different sections: one pertaining to 18th century Venice displayed in the Palazzo Rezzonico, archeology in another wing of the Procuratie Nuove (entered from the Piazzetta), and those we are about to see, again broken up into three departments: History, Paintings, and 19th Century Italian History ("Il Risorgimento").

The Historical Section - In the room leading to the Historical Section is a youthful masterpiece by Antonio Canova, a *statue of Dedalus and Icarus*; the neo-Classical decorative scene is by G. Borsato. The museum, thirty-three rooms in all, contains a vast array of objects and furnishings relating to the history of Venice's institutions art, and social changes. Among the highlights: the *Lion of St. Mark*, flags and emblems of the Republic, portraits and emblems of doges, decrees issued by the doges, descriptions of magnificent public ceremonies, attire worn by doges and high-ranking public officials, relics of the conspiracy led by Bajamonte Tiepolo, superb collections of coins, documents, naval formations, relics of the celebrated Battle of Lepanto, nautical maps and instruments, portraits of the great Venetian explorers and navigators and the great map of their colonial conquests, as well as fascinating weapons, emblems, flags, scepters, and trophies.

The Painting Gallery - This section consists of nineteen superbly decorated rooms on the third floor. For reasons of space we cannot list all the works on display; we shall mention just the highlights in each room. **Room 1,** the Venetian Byzantine school:

A Venetian arsenal.

FV FATTO LANNO 1717 SOTTO MISIER ZACHARIA DANTONIO GASTALDO DE MARANGONI DNAVE D'LARSENA FV RINOVATO D LANNO 1773 SOTTO LA GASTALDIA DI FRANCESCO ZANOTTO GASTALDO E COMPAGNI

in addition to some fine paintings, there is a stupendous 13th century hopechest known as the *Cassa di Beata Giuliana* which shows *Blessed Giuliana with Sts. Biagio and Cataldo.* **Room 2,** 14th century Venetian painting, features works by Paolo Veneziano. **Room 3,** contains works by Lorenzo Veneziano. Of special note is the panel showing *Christ Giving the Keys of the Kingdom to St. Peter* which originally was part of an altarpiece. **Room 4,** the 14th century panel paintings of *Virtues* and the early 14th century *statuette of Doge Tommaso Mocenigo,* by Jacopo Dalle Masegne should not be overlooked. **Room 5,** Venetian High Gothic painting: of major interest are Stefano Veneziano's *Virgin Enthroned* and, in the middle, a 14th century painted *Crucifix.* **Room 6,** Venetian High Gothic painting continued: a fine *Virgin and Child* by Jacobello del Fiore, and altarpiece with *Scenes from the Life of St. Mamante,* by Francesco dei Franceschi, and a *Virgin and Child* by Michele Giambono. **Room 7,** Cosme Tura: displayed are masterpieces by the 15th century painter from Ferrara whose distinctive tormented style produced such remarkable paintings as this *Pietà.* **Room 8,** the Ferrarese School: there are other fine works by Ferrarese artists, as well as two superb *Virgins* by Bartolomeo Vivarini. **Room 9,** contains several Venetian wood sculptures. **Room 10,** the Flemish School paintings, including an *Adoration of the*

Portrait of Doge G. Mocenigo by G. Bellini.

Magi by Pieter Brueghel. **Room 11:** three extraordinary paintings are to be found here: Antonello da Messina's *Pietà* (second half of the 15th century) Hugo Van der Goes' *Crucifixion* and Bouts' *Virgin and Child.* **Room 12,** among the Flemish and German masters displayed are Cranach, Bruyn, and Civetta. **Room 13,** the Bellinis. This family of artists dominated the whole Venetian art world from the early 15th to the beginning of the 16th centuries. Among the masterpieces of two generations of Bellinis here are Jacopo's *Crucifixion,* Gentile's *Portrait of Doge Giovanni Mocenigo* and Giovanni's *Transfiguration, Virgin and Child, Pietà* and a small *Crucifixion.* **Room 14,** Alvise Vivarini and his followers, featuring a superb *St. Anthony of Padua.* **Room 15,** Vittore Carpaccio's most famous painting, the *Courtesans.* **Room 16,** Carpaccio and followers of Bellini, including a fine *Portrait of a Youth with a Red Beret.* **Room 17,** noteworthy are a *Virgin and Child* by Lorenzo Lotto, a *Bust of a Youth* by Giovanni Dalmata, and a *Virgin and Child with saints* by Boccaccino. **Room 18,** the "*Madonneri*" (Greco-Venetian painters of the 16th and 17th centuries). **Room 19,** a collection of 16th century ceramics of incredible beauty and workmanship. The *Servizio Correr,* a service of seventeen pieces decorated by Niccolò Pellipario c. 1525, is particularly noteworthy.

The Risorgimento Museum - This 20-room section is devoted to relics of the period during which the Italians were

The Courtesans, by *V. Carpaccio.*

struggling to attain their national identity and unity. It was set up after Venice was annexed to the Italian state under a bequest made by Piero Marsich, one of the main figures in the heroic but unsuccessful fight against the Austrians in 1848-1849. The rooms illustrate the fall of the Republic of Venice after a millenium of independence, the period of Napoleonic occupation, the Austrian domination, the conspiracies, the defense and surrender of the city in 1849 and finally, the liberation from the Austrians. The exhibit includes flags, relics of the famous patriots (foremost of whom Daniele Manin), weapons, oils and watercolors, as well as documents and photos, all related to the events of the Italian unity movement. A special room has been set aside for another important national struggle, the Resistance to the German occupation, from 1943-1945.

THIRD ITINERARY

• •

Piazzetta di San Marco.

PIAZZETTA DI SAN MARCO

The Piazzetta serves as the simple but elegant antechamber to the grandiose Piazza San Marco. Two of the city's foremost monuments face on to it: the Doges' Palace on the east and the Libreria Sansoviana on the west. Originally a market for foodstuffs occupied this area, but then in 1536 the reigning doge decreed that the space should be kept clear.

By the docks are two monolithic columns (one with the *Lion of St. Mark* and the other with a statue of *St. Theodore*), both brought to Venice from the Orient in 1125. There was supposed to be a third column, but it fell into the water and sank right in front of the quay during transport, and nobody was ever able to retrieve it. The surving two were set up on this spot in 1172 by a certain Niccolò Starantonio who had previously built one of the earliest wooden Rialto Bridges. The authorities rewarded him for his hard work with a license to open up a betting stand in the space between the columns. At the time the rage of the city was a game called "*baratto*" and thus Niccolò received the nickname "*Barattieri*" The statue of St. Theodore (Todardo, in dialect) the first patron saint of Venice, standing atop the column, is actually a collage of different parts from different places, whereas the bronze lion on the second column is believed to be of Eastern, some even claim Chinese, origin. The Piazzetta was also the scene of public executions and between these columns both humble citizens and high-ranking personages were dealt the death sentence. Two of them passed into history. One was Pietro Faziol, known as "*Il Fornaretto*" (the baker's boy) who was executed after being unjustly charged with having killed a nobleman. Since then two oil lamps have been kept burning in his memory on the façade of St. Mark's nearest the Piazzetta. The other was the Count of Carmagnola, charged with high treason and executed on the same spot.

The columns of San Todaro and of the Lion of St. Mark.

The Libreria Sansoviniana.

🏛 LIBRERIA SANSOVINIANA (Library of St. Mark)

The Library takes up the whole west side of the Piazzetta. Considered Sansovino's masterpiece, it was defined as "the most sumptuous ever built" by the architect Palladio, while the writer Pietro Aretino remarked that it "surpasses envy". The construction of a library to house the fabulous collection of rare books donated to the city by Cardinal Bessarione (who had been granted asylum here) was resolved by the Senate of the Republic in 1536.

(Bessarione, an erudite Greek Humanist, had sought refuge in Italy when Nicaea was overrun by the Turks.) The commission was awarded to Jacopo Sansovino, already a well-known architect, who soon went to work on his Classical-style design. But the project got off to a bad start when, in 1545, the ceiling of the half-finished building caved in causing the death of several workmen. Sansovino was actually jailed for this, and only on his release (to a great extent favored by the intercession of Titian, Pietro Aretino, and other famous men) could he go back to the project, though he would never live to see it finished. Following Sansovino's death in 1554, a pupil of his, Vincenzo Scamozzi, took over where the master had left off, and finished the Library, with the addition of the superb façade on the quay side, in 1588. The façade, too, repeats the typically Venetian motif of a ground floor arcade beneath a loggia that we also find in the Procuratie in Piazza San Marco and in the Doges' Palace. Although the style of the building is clearly neo-Classical, and thus extremety different from the Doges' Palace, it in no way clashes with the overall harmony of the Piazzetta. Above the frieze of festoons and cupids running the length of the building is a balcony with statues by various sculptors including Vittoria, Lombardo, and the Tuscan, Ammannati. On either side of the entrance beneath the arcade are two caryatid figures nicknamed "the phenomenal ones", which were sculpted by Vittoria. From here you enter the Library of St. Mark and the Marciana National Library.

In the Library of St. Mark's there is a permanent exhibition featuring a number of rare items including the renowned *Grimani Breviary*, illuminated by late 15th century Flemish masters whereas the Marciana preserves precious Greek and Latin manuscripts.

Enamelled cover of an illuminated manuscript inlaid with precious stones.

THE ARCHEOLOGICAL MUSEUM

An important collection of Classical art is laid out in twenty rooms of the Procuratie Nuove. Begun by Cardinal Domenico Grimani in 1523 and bequeathed by him to the Republic, it is made up of marble and bronze archeological finds from Rome and Greece. It was further expanded by the cardinal's nephew Giovanni Grimani, Patriarch of Aquileia.

Only the highlights of the twenty rooms will be indicated. **Room I** contains an extensive collection of Greek and Roman inscriptions, of special interest for scholars. **Room 2** has four showcases in which a practically complete collection of Roman coins is on display. **Room 3** offers some fine pieces of Greek sculpture including *Hecates* (3rd century B.C.), the *Sosandra Aphrodite* (15th century B.C.) and a *torso of Apollo*. **Room 4** contains outstanding 5-4th century B.C. sculptures: the

Headless Athena, the *Grimani Hera*, and, in the center, the *Persephone* which dates from the time of Phidias. **Room 5** contains Greek and Roman Classical works including *Dionysus and the Satyr* and the celebrated *Grimani Ara* (altar). **Room 7**, of special note are the headless *Aphrodite*, the *funerary stele of tysandra* and the *superb Zulian cameo*, depicting Jupiter, from Ephesus. **Room 8** contains Hellenistic works such as the 3rd century B.C. *Ulysses*, a Roman copy of a Greek original. **Room 9** has a fine collection of Roman portraits ranging from the Republican period to the 3rd century A.D.; those of *Pompeus* and *Vitellius* are especially fine. **Room 10**, Roman portraits continued. **Room 11**, shows Greek and Roman reliefs. In the showcases are ivories and small bronzes. *Room 12, statues of Venus.* **Room 13** *Mithras Sacrificing a Bull.* **Room 14**, a series of finely-crafted vases. **Room 15** contains a fascinating collection of Roman altars, reliefs, and plaques. **Room 16** has re-elaborated pieces of Classical art. **Rooms 17 and 18** display the Egyptian sculpture and Greek reliefs originally in the Correr collection. **Room 19** contains a fine Roman sarcophagus and prehistoric artifacts, and Greek bronzes and ceramics in the showcases. **Room 20**, the Near East collection, has Egyptian mummies and statuettes, and Assyrian reliefs in the showcases.

The name of the architect who designed this remarkable building has been lost, but whoever it was made it the symbol of the supreme power and glory of the Republic of St. Mark. On this site, towards the end of the 9th century, Doges Angelo and Giustiniano Partecipazio established the seat of the government which came to be known as the "Palazzo Ducale" (Doges' Palace), since it was the residence of the Doge, the supreme head of state. However, the impressive structure we see today retains nothing of its 9th century origins. In fact, before the year 1000, when it was a Byzantine palace built over pre-existing Roman walls, the 9th century building was gutted in a fire. It was rebuilt a number of times, until 1340, when it assumed its present-day form. Actually, tradition ascribes the building of the 14th century palace to Filippo Calandario, stone-cutter, Pietro Baseio, and Master Enrico. The façade overlooking the lagoon was completed between 1400-1404, whereas the Piazzetta side was not ready until 1424. Although renowned Florentine and Lombard masters were called in to decorate the prestigious building, most of the ornamental design in the elaborate Flamboyant Gothic style was handled by a Venetian family of artists who were highly skilled marble craftsmen, the Bons. The result is this incredible building, seemingly suspended over the double tier of arcading which gives it such an airy effect. Then in 1577 another fire broke out, burning down an entire wing. Another competition for its reconstruction was announced and entries from the most celebrated architects of the day poured in. The project by Antonio Da Ponte, architect of the Rialto Bridge, was selected and the building was restored to its 14th century appearance.

The Doges' Palace.

THE FAÇADES

A person approaching the palace from the canal perceives it like a fairytale mirage, with its delicate pink and white patterned walls and its seemingly weightless architectural structure. The façade is symmetrically broken up by the lovely carved balcony built by Pier Paolo and Jacobello Dalle Masegne in true Flamboyant Gothic style (that is, with elaborate sculptural decoration). Rising above the whole is a statue of Venice in the Robes of Justice, a 16th century work by Alessandro Vittoria. Worthy of attention amongst the elegant carved capitals of the arcade columns is the first one on the Piazzetta side representing *Adam and Eve in the Garden of Eden* (early 15th century). The west façade facing the Piazzetta closely resembles the south (canal) side, with a balcony erected by pupils of Sansovino in 1536 imitating the one designed by the Dalle Massegnes. Over the pointed arch window is a panel with Doge Andrea Gritti before the symbol of Venice, a modern work by Ugo Bonasso, and, on the very top, a statue of Justice by Alessandro Vittoria.

Left: **the balcony on the western façade of the Doges' Palace**, *school of Sansovino*, **with the statue of Venice in the Robes of Justice**, by *A. Vittoria*, and **the statue of the Doge Andrea Gritti before the Symbol of Venice**, by *U. Botasso*.

The Doges' Palace seen from the Grand Canal; below, *the Judgement of Solomon,*
marble group at the corner of the Doges' Palace attributed to *Pietro Lamberti*
or *Nanni di Bartolo.*

Right by the façade of the church of St. Mark on the Piazzetta side is the so-called **Porta della Carta**, literally the Charter Portal, to which government decrees were affixed. It originally was known as the "golden portal", since it was once decorated in blue and gold. The upper section, elaborately carved as befits the Flamboyant Gothic taste, is the work of the Bon family. Just above the doorway is a statue of *Doge Foscari Kneeling before the Winged Lion* (modern), while the woman seated above the tallest spire represents *Justice.* On the corner of the Doges' Palace is a famous sculptural group depicting the *Judgement of Solomon.* This extraordinary 15th century sculpture has been attributed to either Pietro Lamberti or Nanni di Bartolo.

The courtyard of the Doges' Palace.
Preceding page: ***the Porta della Carta,*** *surmounted by the statue of Doge Francesco Foscari before the Winged Lion.*

● THE INTERIOR

Now that the damage caused by the popular uprising of 1797 at the time of the French occupation has been repaired, the interior of the Doges' Palace and all of the art masterpieces it contains have been restored to their former splendor. Here for hundreds of years the Doges and high-ranking officials of the Republic vied in accumulating extraordinary pieces to adorn these rooms in which the most important decisions regarding the life of the city were made. Today, all kinds of cultural events are held inside the palace itself or in the courtyard, which makes a unique setting for the nighttime concerts held throughout summer.

THE COURTYARD

The Porta della Carta brings us to the **Foscari Portico** which we cross to enter the courtyard of the Doges' Palace. Its effect is both peaceful and majestic. In the middle is a pair of imposing bronze well-curbs. The one closer to the portal is by Alfonso Alberghetti (1559), while the other is by Niccolò dei Conti (1556), both of whom worked as cannon forgers for the Republic of St. Mark. The main or eastern façade (facing the entrance) was designed by Antonio Rizzo at the end of the 15th century. Its pleasing esthetic effect is largely a result of the harmony of the architectural elements achieved by combining the lower, Gothic, section with the upper, Renaissance, level. If you think about it, such bold blending of different styles is a hallmark of Venetian architecture and one of the reasons for its special charm. The elaborate decorative scheme is by Pietro Lombardo (15th century). The right side was designed by Scarpagnino in the mid 1500s, whereas the two brick façades which border the courtyard on the

97

The Renaissance wing of the courtyard; below: *the Staircase of the Giants.*

south and west sides were built by Bartolomeo Manopola in the 17th century as imitations of the outer façades. The arches of the north façade, on top of which is a giant clock, are broken up by niches with restored Antique statues inside them, another Baroque creation by Manopola. To the right, set on a tall base, is a *monument to Francesco Maria I della Rovere,* Duke of Urbino sculpted by Giovanni Bandini in 1587. By the Staircase of the Giants is the **Foscari Arch,** begun by the Bons in the Gothic style, and later finished by Rizzo and the Bregnos according to the Renaissance taste. Along the top of the structure are *statues of St. Mark* and other allegorical figures. The niches

The statues of Mars and Neptune by *Sansovino;* below: *two bronze well curbs* by *Niccolò dei Conti* and *Alfonso Alberhetti.*

below contain *statues of Adam and Eve,* bronze copies of Antonio Rizzo's originals now inside the palace. Alongside the Staircase of the Giants is the tiny **Courtyard of the Senators** where the senators of the Republic supposedly assembled during official ceremonies. The **Staircase of the Giants** received its name from the two colossal *statues of Mars and Neptune* on either side of the landing. The statues are by Sansovino and his pupils; the overall project, however, was designed by Antonio Rizzo at the end of the 15th century. The new doges were officially crowned on the landing at the top of the stairs. Having climbed the staircase we are on the second floor loggia.

99

FIRST PIANO NOBILE

1. The Scala d'Oro - Golden Staircase
2. Scarlatti Room
3. Shield Room
4. Grimani Room
5. Erizzo Room
6. Stucco Room
7. Philosphers' Room
8. The Doge's private apartments (Painting Collection)
9. Room of the Quarantia Criminal
10. Anteroom of the Maggior Consiglio
11. Room of the Qarantia Civil Vecchia
12. Guariento Room
13. Room of the Great Council
14. Room of the Quarantia Civil Nuova
15. Voting Room
16. Room of the Censors

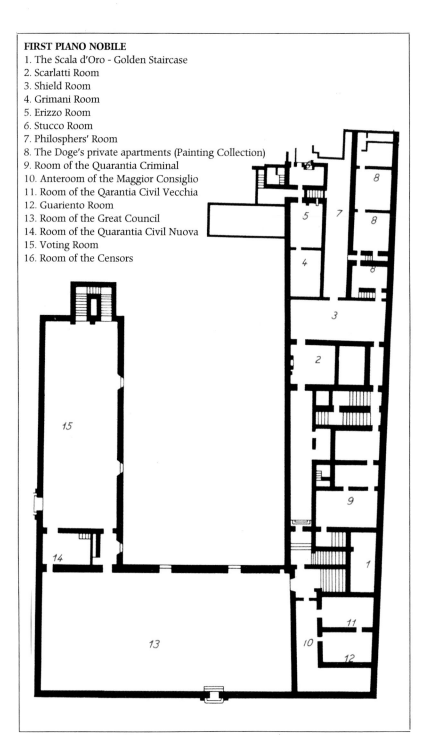

The Scarlatti Room.

THE SECOND FLOOR (OR PIANO NOBILE)

To reach the upper floors of the palace we take the **Scala d'Oro**, literally, the Golden Staircase, designed by Sansovino in 1538 for Doge Andrea Gritti, but completed by Scarpagnino in 1559. The staircase, with a barrel vault ceiling covered with splendid gilded stucco reliefs was originally reserved for the VIPs of the day. The first arch at the entrance is decorated with two sculptures by Tiziano Aspetti (2nd half of the 16th century) portraying *Hercules* and *Atlas*. Two statues by Francesco Segala symbolizing *Abundance* and *Charity* decorate the third floor. The second floor, which served as the doges' private apartments, was first occupied by Doge Agostino Barbarigo towards the end of the 15th century, as it had to be completely rebuilt after the 1483 fire (the architects commissioned were Antonio Rizzo and Pietro Lombardo).

The Sala degli Scarlatti (the Scarlatti Room) - The room received its name since all of the high-ranking members of the doge's entourage wore scarlet on official occasions. The splendid ceiling decoration of a gold pattern against a blue ground was executed by Biagio and Pietro da Faenza in 1505. The Lombardos sculpted the fireplace on which you can see the coat-of-arms of the Barbarigo family. The stucco relief depicting the *Virgin and Child* is a Paduan school work. Opposite is a relief representing *Doge Leonardo Loredan Presented to the Virgin by St. Mark*, that shows the influence of Pietro Lombardo's style.

Preceding page: *The Scala d'Oro - Golden Staircase.*
Right: *Room of the Maps, or of the Shield*

The Sala dello Scudo (the Shield Room) - The shield belonging to Venice's last doge was preserved here and thus the room's name. In addition, it once served as an assembly hall for the doge's private guards. The maps around it were made in 1762 by F. Grisellini who based himself on existing maps made prior to 1540.

The Sala Grimani (the Grimani Room) - In the center of the ceiling is the coat-of-arms of the Grimani family after whom the room was named. The painted frieze just below the ceiling, which has been attributed to Andrea Vicentino, consists of panels with allegorical scenes. The marble fireplace was sculpted at the beginning of the 16th century by Tullio and Antonio Lombardo.

The Sala Erizzo (the Erizzo Room) - On the fireplace is the coat-of-arms of Doge Erizzo. The carved ceiling dates from the 16th century. From the adjoining terrace, transformed into a hanging garden, there is a fine view over the courtyard.

The Sala degli Stucchi (the Stucco Room) - The stucco decoration dates from the time of the dogeship of Marino Grimani. Several noteworthy paintings are hanging here: an *Adoration of the Magi* by Bonifacio de' Pitati, a *Portrait of Henry III* by Tintoretto, an *Adoration of the Shepherds* by Leandro Bassano, and a *Holy Family* by Salviati.

The Sala dei Filosofi (the Philosophers' Room) - Twelve portraits of philosophers by Veronese and Tintoretto, now in Sansovino's Library, originally hung here. A long corridor leads to the doge's private chapel whose door is adorned with a *St. Christopher,* a fine work by Titian.

The Lion of St. Mark, by *V. Carpaccio* (Picture Gallery).

The Painting Collection - These three rooms, once part of the doge's private suite, overlook the little canal behind the Doges' Palace. Noteworthy are the 15th century fireplaces with the Barbarigo coat-of-arms, part of elaborate decorative schemes. In the rooms are paintings once hung elsewhere in the palace. The first one contains a *Lamentation* by Giovanni Bellini and, facing it, Carpaccio's famous *Lion of St. Mark* painted in 1516, which has an interesting view of the harbor of St. Mark's in the background. In the second room are paintings by the famous 16th century Flemish painter, Bosch. The two panel paintings represent *Heaven* and *Hell,* while the subjects of the two altarpieces are the *Temptation of Sts. Jerome, Anthony and Egidius* and the *Martyrdom of St. Juliana.* These paintings called "*stregozzi*" (literally, spellbinders) are typical products of Bosch's striking imaginative genius. In the third room is a *Virgin and Child* by Boccaccino and a *Lamentation* by Antonello da Saliba.

The Sala degli Scudieri (the Squires' Room) - This room is reached through the Map Room. The fine works on display include *Venice Receiving the Homage of Neptune* by Tiepolo, the *Annunciation* by Palma the Younger, and three allegorical paintings by Domenico Tintoretto.

We retrace our steps to the Scala d'Oro and go up a flight. The third floor occupies the whole east wing of the building and was rebuilt over a long period after being destroyed by fire.

The Atrio Quadrato (the Square Atrium) - The octagonal painting in the center of the carved wooden ceiling of *Doge Gerolamo Priuli Receiving the Sword and Scales from Justice* by Tintoretto shows the master's skill in achieving striking compositional and coloristic effects. Two of the several noteworthy paintings displayed here are *Adam and Eve* and the *Prayer in the Garden*, both by Paolo Veronese.

The Sala delle Quattro Porte (the Room of the Four Doors) - This was once the assembly hall of the Collegio (Council), but it later served as a special anteroom to the Senate Chamber. Built by Antonio Da Ponte after a design by Andrea Palladio, it has elaborate gold and white stucco decoration. The subjects of the paintings are allegorical representations of the power and glory of the Venetian republic. Of special note are the allegorical ceiling frescos by Tintoretto and the celebrated painting of *Doge Antonio Grimani Kneeling before Faith in the Presence of St. Mark* by Titian.

The Anticollegio (the Antechamber) - People waiting to be received by the doge assembled here. On the ceiling is *Venice Distributing Honors and Rewards* by Veronese. The elaborate fireplace was designed by Vincenzo Scamozzi. Four masterpieces by Tintoretto adorn the walls: *Vulcan's Forge, Mercury and the Three Graces, Bacchus and Ariadne,* and *Minerva Dismissing Mars.* Veronese painted the much-restored *Rape of Europa.*

The Lion of St. Mark, by *V. Carpaccio* (Picture Gallery).

Vulcan's Forge (above) and *the Ariadne, Bacchus and Venus* (below), two paintings by *J. Tintoretto* (Anteroom).

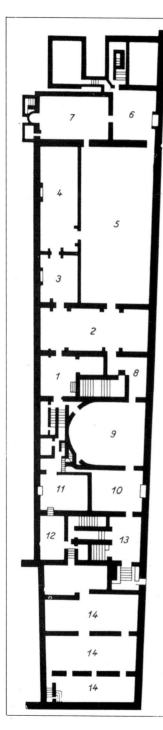

SECOND PIANO NOBILE

1. Square Atrium
2. Room of the Four Doors
3. Antechamber
4. Council Chamber
5. Senate Chamber
6. Chapel Antechamber
7.Chapel
8. Corridor
9. Room of the Council of Ten
10. Compass Room
11. Room of the Heads of the Council of Ten
12. Inquisitors' Room
13. Staircase of the Censors, landing.
14. Salles d'Armes of the Council of Ten.

The Sala del Collegio (the Council Chamber) - This is where the doge and the highranking magistrates held audiences and discussed affairs of state. The room was designed by Palladio and built by Da Ponte. On the ceiling is a superb cycle of paintings by Veronese whose skillful treatment of light and harmonious compositional patterns create particularly attractive effects. The subjects of these allegorical paintings are the *Allegory of Faith* (center), *Sacrifice* (below), *Venice Enthroned Crowned by Justice and Peace* (above the tribune), *Mars and Neptune* (above the entrance), and a series of allegorical figures. On the tribune wall is the *Glorification of the Victory of Lepanto* by Veronese, while paintings by Jacopo Tintoretto complete the decorative scheme.

Council Chamber.

The Sala del Senato (the Senate Chamber) - Here the doge presided over the senate meetings. The subjects of the paintings are all related to the glorification of Venice and her rulers. On the ceiling is Tintoretto's *Venice, Queen of the Seas* and, over the doge's throne, two other Tintorettos, the *Dead Christ* and *Doge Loredan Praying to the Virgin to End the Famine and Concede a Victory over the Turks*. Above the door opposite the throne is a painting by Palma the Younger depicting *Doges Lorenzo and Girolamo Priuli Praying the Savior to End the Plague*. The senators' seats were restored in the 18th century.

The Doge Pietro Loredan Imploring the Virgin to End the Famine, by J. Tinoretto; below: **the Senate Chamber.**

The Antichiesetta (the Chapel Antechamber) - The ceiling of this stuccoed room has frescoes by Guarana representing *Allegories of Good Government*. On the walls are the cartoons done by Sebastiano Ricci for the façade of St. Mark's, showing the *Arrival of the Body of St. Mark in Venice.*

Room of the Council of Ten.

The Chiesetta (the Chapel) - It was built by Vincenzo Scamozzi in 1593. On the altar is a sculpture of the *Virgin and Child with St. John* by Jacopo Sansovino and on the ceiling are frescoes by Guarana.

The Sala del Consiglio dei Dieci (the Room of the Council of Ten) - In this room the much-feared Ten (magistrates) who were entrusted with security of state held their meetings. The subjects of the paintings all pertain to the council's functions. In the center of the ceiling is a copy of a Veronese, *Jupiter Smiting Vices.* The original carried off by the French in 1797, is presently in the Louvre. The *Old man in Eastern Dress with a Girl* and *Juno Offers the*

Doges' Hat to Venice are by Veronese. In the other compartments are allegorical figures by Ponchino and Zelotti.

The Sala della Bussola (the Compass Room) - The "*compass*" is actually the double door leading to the adjoining Sala dei Capi del Consiglio dei Dieci. Here people about to be questioned and the condemned were kept waiting. Along one of the walls you can still see the notorious "*bocche di leone*" (literally, lions' mouths), actually slots into which citizens could drop anonymous denunciations. The fireplace is by Sansovino and his helpers. On the ceiling is a copy of a Veronese, *St. Mark and the Virtues*, the original of which is in the Louvre.

The Sala dei Tre Capi del Consiglio dei Dieci (the Room of the Three Heads of the Council of Ten) - Of special note are two paintings by Veronese, the *Punishment of the Forger* and *Sin Vanquished by Victory* and the fireplace by Jacopo Sansovino.

The Saletta degli Inquisitori (the Inquisitors' Room) - In this room (which directly communicates with the prisons) people were brought before the Inquisition for questioning. The ceiling paintings are by Tintoretto.

The Landing of the Censors' Staircase - Retracing our steps through the Compass Room we come out by the staircase leading up to the Weapons Rooms.

Left: *Room of the Heads of the Council of Ten*; below: *the Compass Room.*

The Sale d'Armi del Consiglio dei Dieci (the Salles d'Armes Rooms of the Council of Ten)
- In the past these rooms were used as prisons, but starting from the early 14th century, they were turned into armories. Today they contain a fascinating, easy-to-follow collection of weapons of the past. The objects on display comprise swords (one of which is an especially fine example of 14th century Venetian craftsmanship), pikes, halberds, armor (including the armor worn by Henry IV King of France and two suits of armor that once belonged to the Sforza family), and a twenty-barrel arquebus. Among the sculptures are a marble *bust of Sebastiano Venier*, the hero of the Battle of Lepanto, by Alessandro Vittoria, a *bronze bust of Francesco Morosini* by the Genoese artist Filiberto Parodi, and a *bronze bust of Marcantonio Bragadin* by Tiziano Aspetti.

We return, by way of the Scala dei Censori, to the second floor (where we have already visited the doge's private apartments). We shall now tour the remaining rooms.

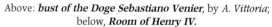

Above: **bust of the Doge Sebastiano Venier**, by *A. Vittoria*; below, **Room of Henry IV.**

The Andito del Maggior Consiglio (the Corridor of the Great Council) - This hallway overlooking the harbor is illuminated by beautiful Gothic windows. On the right wall are works by Palma the Younger; on the left, works by Tintoretto.

The Sala della Quarantia Civil Vecchia (the Room of the Forty) - This room was the seat of the Supreme Court composed of forty members. It too is adorned with allegorical and commemorative paintings.

The Sala del Guariento (the Guariento Room) - Originally it was called the Armament Room as ammunition was stored here, but now it contains what is left of a masterpiece of art, the *Paradise* fresco by the 14th century Paduan artist, Guariento, which was originally painted for the Sala del Maggior Consiglio. Damaged in the fire of 1577, it was replaced by a painting of the same subject commissioned from Jacopo Tintoretto in 1580. We can appreciate its great beauty from this *Coronation of the Virgin,* peopled with figures of angels, saints, and prophets.

The Sala del Maggior Consiglio (the Hall of the Great Council) - This incredibly huge hall (it measures 177 feet long, 82 feet wide, and 50 feet high) was used for meetings of the Great Council, the Republic's governing body. Five huge Gothic windows looking out on the harbor, two on the Piazzetta, and two on the courtyard afford splendid views over the lagoon and all the famous sights in the vicinity. After the 1577 fire which destroyed the original hall that had been officially inaugurated by Doge Francesco Foscari in 1423, it was soon rebuilt by Antonio Da Ponte and decorated with

Room of the Quarantia Civil Vecchia.

Room of the Maggior Consiglio.

iconography created by a Florentine scholar, Girolamo de' Bardi and the Venetian historian, F. Sansovino. Upon entering you are immediatety struck by the huge painting above the tribune (measuring 72x22 feet). It represents *Paradise* and was painted by Tintoretto between 1588 and 1590. Although numerous restorations have marred a good deal of the original light and shade contrasts, nothing can harm the impressive monumentality of the compositional pattern. Christ and the Virgin are surrounded by saints artfully placed to mark the picture planes. The overwhelming ceiling composed of thirty-five compartments set in grandiose gilded frames was put up by Cristoforo Sorte between 1578 and 1584. Turning our backs to the platform, we shall now examine the highlights of the ceiling paintings, starting from the ones by the harbor wall and then passing to the right side and back to the Door of the Quarantia Civil Nova. 1 - *Antonio Loredan Commands the Attack to Free Scutari from the Siege of Mohammed II,* by Paolo Veronese. 2 - *The Venetian Army and Navy Conquer Polesella,* by Francesco Bassano. 3 - *Vittore Soranzo and His Fleet Victorious at Argenta* (1482) *against the Troops of Ercole I d'Este,* by Jacopo Tintoretto and his helpers. 4 - *Jacopo Marcello's Conquest of Gallipoli* (1494), by Tintoretto. 5 - *Giorgio Cornaro and Bartolo Defeating the Imperial Troops of Maximilian I at Cadore,* by Francesco Bassano. 6 - *Andrea Gritti Reconquering Padua,* by Palma the Younger. 7 - In the oval, *Venice Crowned by Victory Welcomes the Vanquished Peoples and Conquered Provinces,* by Palma the Younger. 8 - In the main panel, *Venice Surrounded by Sea Divinities Hands an Olive Branch to Doge Niccolò Da Ponte,* by Tintoretto. 9 - In the oval, *Apotheosis of Venice,* by Veronese. 10 (courtyard side) - *Pietro Mocenigo Leading the Venetians to Victory at Castelmaggiore,* by Francesco Bassano. 11 - *Stefano Contarini Defeating the Visconti Navy at Riva in 1440*, by Tintoretto. 12 - *The Venetians Led by Francesco Barbaro Helping the City of Brescia Break the Siege of Filippo Maria Visconti*, by Tintoretto. 13 - *Carmagnola Leading the Venetians to Victory at Maclodio in 1426*, by Francesco Bassano. 14 - *Francesco Bembo Leading the Po Fleet to Victory over Visconti's Troops in Cremona*, by Palma the Younger. The portraits of doges just beneath the ceiling are by Domenico Tintoretto and his helpers. There is also an empty space covered by a black cloth with a Latin inscription that reads: "This is the place of Marin Faliero, beheaded for his crimes" (high treason). The subjects of the paintings along the court-

yard wall are related to the struggle between Pope Alexander III and Frederick Barbarossa in which Venice was politically involved. The most interesting are *the Ambassadors Petitioning Barbarossa for Peace*, by fol-

Room of the Quarantia Civil Nuova; below: **the Venetian Fleet Prepares to Sail Against Barbarossa**, by *F. Bassano* (Room of the Great Council).

lowers of Tintoretto (fourth panel from the far side of the room), *the Pope Handing the Sword to the Doge* (fifth panel), and *Frederick Barbarossa Prostrate Before the Pope by Federico* (tenth panel).

The Sala della Quarantia Civil Nuova (the Room of the Civil Court Forty) - This was the seat of the appeals court for citizens residing on the mainland. The fine gilded beam ceiling dates from the 1500s. Above the tribune, partially lined with gilded leather, on which the various judges' coats-of-arms are embossed, is a 15th century *Virgin* against a gold ground. The paintings along the walls represent *Venice and Justice,* by A. Foler, *Venice and Neptune, the Virtues,* and *Justice expelling the Vices,* by G. B. Lorenzetti, and *Justice and Time Strip Truth Naked,* by F. Zaniberti.

The Sala dello Scrutinio (the Voting Room) - Starting in 1532, this room was where ballots were cast for the election of the Great Council and where commissioners for the election of the doge met. Before the 1577 fire its walls were adorned with paintings by Tintoretto and Pordenone. After being restored by Antonio Da Ponte in 1587, the great hall was redecorated. The theme of the paintings commissioned was once more the glorification of Venice's triumphs on the high seas, drawn up by erudite scholars. Again, not being able to list each and every work, we shall give only the highlights. In the elaborate gilded ceiling attributed to Sorte is the *Conquest of Padua* by Francesco Bassano; on the entrance wall the *Last Judgement* by Palma the Younger; on the courtyard wall the *Conquest of Zara* by Tintoretto and his helpers, and, above the windows, the *Battle of Lepanto,* by Andrea Vicentino. Beneath the ceiling are portraits of doges, a continuation of the series

The Voting Room.

started in the Sala del Maggior Consiglio. The balcony affords a splendid view over the Piazzetta and the Basilica of St. Mark. At the far end of the room is a grandiose *Triumphal Arch,* inspired by Classical Roman models, which was built in honor of Doge Francesco Morosini by Antonio Tirali (attribution).

The Sala della Quarantia Criminal (the Room of the Crimmal Court Forty) - Reached from the Censors' Staircase, the room contains a noteworthy *Lion of St. Mark* by Jacobello del Fiore.

The Sala del Magistrato al Criminal and the Sala del Magistrato alle Leggi (the Room of the Criminal Court Magistrate and the Room of the Law Magistrate) - Antonio Rizzio's original marble sculptures of *Adam and Eve* (dated 1470), once in the Foscari Arch of the courtyard, have been placed here.

Interior of one of the "Pozzi" cells.

1629) and portraits of several of them by Tintoretto and Palma.

The Sala dei Notai or Sala dell'Avogaria (the Room of the Magistrates) - The walls are hung with portraits of famous *notai* and *avogadori* and several religious scenes by Leandro Bassano and Tintoretto's followers. On one of the walls hangs an odd clock with only six hours shown on its face. The *Avogaria* was in charge of the so-called Gold and Silver Books, kept in the adjoining Sala dello Scrigno, which listed the noble families of the city.

The Prisons - By the Scala d'Oro, on the east side of the Loggias, is a small door which leads to the prisons and the Bridge of Sighs, which communicated with the Avogaria (magistrates' offices) and other courts. The prisoners were led before their judges via the Bridge of Sighs. Prior to the construction of the Palazzo delle Prigioni (Prison Building), this was known as the Old Prison. It was composed of two sections: the *Piombi* (literally, lead) whose cells were located under a lead roof and the *Pozzi* (wells), dank and dark dungeons below the level of the lagoon in which the most dangerous criminals were kept. The eighteen cells making up the pozzi may be visited by descending a flight of stairs.

We shall now visit the suite of rooms known as the **Avogaria** in the east wing of the Doges' Palace on the same floor as the loggias.

The Sala dei Censori (the Room of the Censors) - The room served as offices for the two *censori* whose job it was to watch over the mores of the nobles and denounce cheating in elections. Around the walls are the coats-of-arms of 266 *censori* (from 1517 to

The Sala della Milizia da Mar (the Room of the Militia of the Sea) - This was the headquarters for the captains in charge of recruiting men for the fleet of the Serenissima. The walls are decorated with 18th century frescoes in Tiepolo's style, one of which, the *Adoration of the Magi* has been attributed to Gian Domenico Tiepolo himself. A small adjoining room once served as the office of the *Segretario alle voci* (literally, Secretary of the Items) who was in charge of recording the names of those awarded public office.

Entrance to the New Prisions.

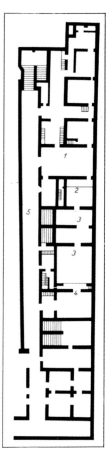

Palace of the New Prisions; below: *the Ponte della Paglia.*

THE LOGGIA FLOOR
1. The Doges' Chancellery
2. Room of the Militia of the Sea
3. Room of the Magistrates
4. Room of the Censors
5. Golden Staircase
6. Loggia.

The Sala della Cancelleria Ducale (the Doges' Chancellery) - This room, where the Collegio dei Notai held its meetings, was the office of the Head Chancellor. From here a staircase descends to the pozzi which we have previously described.

The Museo dell'Opera di Palazzo (the Doges' Palace Museum) - The ground floor museum is well worth a visit. Exhibited here are the original capitals from the palace's outside colonnade, many of which had to be replaced for restoration, as well as columns, reliefs, several original pieces of crenellation, and the original architrave from the Porta della Carta by Bartolomeo Bon.

As soon as our tour of the Doges' Palace is over we return to the Piazzetta and turning left, walk down to the docks where we enjoy a glorious view of the harbor. To the left, along the southern side of the Palace, we come to the **Ponte della Paglia** (Straw Bridge), perhaps nicknamed for the barges transporting straw for the prisons which docked here. It was built in 1360 and then enlarged in the 19th century. On one of the pylons, facing outwards, is an image of the gondoleers' protectress, *Our Lady of the Gondoleers,* set inside a 16th century tabernacle.

The Bridge of Sighs.

THE BRIDGE OF SIGHS

From the canal side of the Ponte della Paglia you are looking straight at the famous covered bridge, Ponte dei Sospiri, which connects the Doges' Palace and the Prigioni Nuove. Commissioned by Doge Marino Grimano, it was built by Antonio Contini at the turn of the 17th century in the typical Baroque style of the day. The name *"Bridge of Sighs"* presumably derives from the sighs of the prisoners who had to cross it as they were being brought before the Inquisitors.

FOURTH ITINERARY

• •

THE MERCERIE

Although its names are multiple - Merceria dell'Orologio, Merceria di San Zulian, Merceria del Capitello, Merceria di San Salvador, and Merceria del Due Aprile - "*Le Mercerie*" actually refers to a single street right in the heart of the city perenially thronged with a colorful crowd of natives and out-of-towners shopping or just windowshopping. In fact, the street, entered from the arch beneath the Clocktower in Piazza San Marco, was named for the "*merci*" (wares) which are its main attraction.

Just a short way ahead on the **Campo San Zulian** is the **church of San Giuliano**. The church building is much older than the façade with its two rows of semi-columns surmounted by a tympanum which was erected in 1553 by Jacopo Sansovino and Alessandro Vittoria. The *statue of Tommaso Rangone,* the benefactor of the church has been attributed to Vittoria. Inside is a fine *Pietà* by Girolamo Campagna and several works by Palma the Younger.

Taking the **Merceria Zan Zulian** and continuing along the **Merceria del Capitello**, and then the **Merceria San Salvador** we come to **Campo San Salvador** and the church of the same name.

Campo San Salvador.

THE CHURCH OF SAN SALVADOR

Although this is one of the oldest churches in Venice, it has been remodeled over the centuries, first in the 16th century by Giorgio Spavento, then by Tullio Lombardo, and lastly by Sansovino and Scamozzi, who gave it its present appearance. The intricate carved Baroque façade was designed in 1663 by Bernardino Falcone.

● THE INTERIOR

Not only one of the finest extant examples of Venetian Renaissance architecture this single-naved church is also filled with masterpieces of art. Between the second and third altars of the right aisle is the *tomb monument to Doge Francesco Venier* with statues of *Charity* and *Hope* by Sansovino. A grandiose painting of the *Annunciation* by Titian (1566) adorns the third altar. The main altar contains an

embossed silver altar frontal, a superb example of 14th century Venetian craftsmanship. It is surmounted by a *Transfiguration* by Titian. In the chapel to the left of the main chapel is the *Supper at Emmaus*, recently attributed to Giovanni Bellini. In the left-hand transept is a *monument to the Correr family* by Bernardo Contino.

Retracing our way back through the Mercerie, we return to Campo Zulian. Taking **Calle della Guerra** on the left and then **Calle delle Bande**, we come out

The church of Santa Maria Formosa on the "campo" of the same name.

on **Campo Maria Formosa,** of interest not just because of the lovely buildings around it, but also because it is a picturesque marketplace. Although the original **church of Santa Maria Formosa** was erected much earlier, it was rebuilt by Mauro Coducci in 1492. It has two 16th century façades and a 17th century Baroque belfry. In the shape of a Latin cross, it has no aisles. In the first chapel on the right is a superb *triptych* by Bartolomeo Vivarini. The scenes depicted are the *Nativity of the Virgin*, the *Virgin of Mercy,* and the *Meeting of Joachim and St. Anne*. In the right transept is a renowned altarpiece, *St. Barbara and Four Saints,* painted by Palma the Elder in 1509.

THE QUERINI-STAMPALIA MUSEUM

The Querini Palace, which also houses the **Venice Public Library**, is located right behind the church of Santa Maria Formosa on Calle Querini. The picture gallery, featuring Venetian masters from the 14th-18th centuries, occupies twenty rooms on the second floor. The collection also includes rare furniture, china, arms and armor, as well as musical instruments.

Room 1, contains curious paintings of *Life in Venice* by Gabriele Bella. **Room 2**, the *Coronation of the Virgin*, by Catarino and Donato Veneziano. **Room 3**, *portraits*, by Sebastiano Bombelli. **Room 4**, works by Palma the Younger, including *Adam and Eve* and a *Self-Portrait*. **Rooms 6** and **7**, works by Venetian Mannerists, including *landscapes*, by Matteo de' Pitocchi. **Rooms 8** and **9**, the Renaissance. The highlights here are the *Adoration of the Virgin*, by Lorenzo di Credi, *Sacra Conversazione*, by Palma the Elder, the *Virgin and Child* and *Presentation at the Temple*, by Giovanni Bellini, and *Judith*, by Vincenzo Catena. **Rooms 11-13**, works by Pietro Longhi including the *Seven Sacraments, Hunt in the Valley*, and other genre paintings. **Room 14**, Marco Ricci's *landscapes*. **Room 15** through **20**, drawings by Giovanni Bellini Titian, Raphael, Tintoretto, Veronese, and other masters, in addition to Flemish tapestries, wall hangings, objets d'art, weapons, ceramics, and Louis XVI lacquered furniture. **Room 18**, *Portrait of G. Querini*, by G. Battista Tiepolo. **Room 20**, *Virgin and Child*, by Bernardo Strozzi.

From the Campo Santa Maria Formosa we take the **Calle Lunga** and, practically at the end of it, turn left into **Calle Pinelli**. After crossing the **Rio San Giovanni** we turn left into the **Fondamenta Fozzi** and then right into the **Calle Bressano** until we come out in **Campo Santi Giovanni e Paolo** which, after Piazza San Marco, is the most impressive of the Venetian campi. Overlooking the square are the façades of the church of Santi Giovanni e Paolo and the Scuola Grande di San Marco, with the adjoining **church of San Lazzaro dei Mendicanti**. In the middle is the *equestrian monument to Bartolomeo Colleoni*, condottiere (captain) of the Republic. This masterpiece of Renaissance art was begun, by the Florentine artist Andrea del Verrocchio (1488), also renowned as Leonardo da Vinci's teacher. When Verrocchio died it was finished by Alessandro Leopardi, who is also responsible for the statue's elegant pedestal (1496).

Equestrian monument to Bartolomeo Colleoni, by A.Verrocchio.

The church of San Zanipolo.

 # THE CHURCH OF SS. GIOVANNI E PAOLO (or SAN ZANIPOLO)

Started by the Dominican friars in 1246, it was not finished until 1430. Like its Franciscan counterpart, Santa Maria Gloriosa dei Frari, it is an outstanding example of the architectural style known as Venetian Gothic. Inside are the mortal remains of some of the Serenissima's best-known figures. The façade, a combination of Gothic (Byzantine sculpture) and Renaissance (the elaborate carved portal by Bartolomeo Bon), was never finished.

THE INTERIOR

It is in the form of a Latin cross with a single aisle and a cluster of five apses. Around the doorway are three tombs of members of the Mocenigo family, the finest of which was built for Doge Pietro Mocenigo by Pietro Lombardo in 1485 (on the right). Starting at the first altar of the right aisle is a *Virgin and Saints* by Francesco Bissolo and at the second the *San Vincenzo Ferreri Altarpiece* by Giovanni Bellini (1465). After the **Chapel of Our Lady of Sorrows**, which leads to the **Baptistry**, we come to the *Monument to the Valier Family Doges* by Andrea Tirali (18th century). At the end of the aisle is an elaborately decorated chapel, dedicated to St. Dominic, whose ceiling fresco representing *St. Dominic in Glory* is one of the masterpieces of Piazzetta (1727). In the right transept *Jesus Carrying the Cross* by Alvise Vivarini, *St. Anthony and the Poor* by Lorenzo Lotto (1542) and, by the second altar, *Christ and Saints* by Rocco Marconi. The 15th century Gothic window by Bartolomeo Vivarini is truly magnificent. The choir: conveys a majestic effect with its lightfilled polygonal apse and Baroque main altar. On the right is the 14th century *Monument to Doge Michele Morosini*, with a mosaic

The interior of the church of San Zanipolo.

123

Crucifixion and, a bit further on, the *monument to Doge Leonardo Loredan* of 1572. To the left are monuments to two other doges, *Doge Andrea Vendramin* by Pietro and *Tullio Lombardo* (15th century) and *Doge Marco Corner with a statue of the Virgin* by Nino Pisano. At the far side of the left transept is a *monument to Doge Antonio Venier* by the Dalle Masegnes and below it is the entrance to the 16th century **Chapel of the Rosary**, once adorned with sculpture by Alessandro Vittoria and paintings by Tintoretto, Bassano, and others (it unfortunately perished in a fire in 1867). The reconstructed ceiling contains three works by Veronese: the *Annunciation,* the *Assumption,* and the *Adoration of the Shepherds.* Along the walls are 18th century sculptures and a pair of bronze *candlesticks* by Alessandro Vittoria. From the left aisle we enter the elegant **Sacristy** adorned with paintings by Palma the Younger. Continuing on, funerary *monuments to Doge Pasquale Malipiero* by Pietro Lombardo, *Senator Bonzi, Doge Tommaso Mocenigo* by 15th century Florentine artists, and, lastly, *Niccolò Marcello* by Pietro Lombardo. A *statue of St. Jerome* by Alessandro Vittoria adorns the first altar.

Scuola Grande di San Marco; below: *detail of the façade.*

Interior of the Scuola Grande di San Marco.

The façade of the Scuola Grande di San Marco faces into the **Campo San Zanipolo**, while a side overlooks the **Rio dei Mendicanti**, a charming canal. The Venetian "*scuole*" were religious congregations, mostly founded around the mid-1200s by the Franciscan and Dominican orders, to perform charity.

Details of the façade of the Scuola Grande di San Marco.

THE SCUOLA GRANDE DI SAN MARCO
(School of St. Mark)

Established in 1437, it was burnt down in a fire and completely rebuilt by Pietro Lombardo and Mauro Coducci from 1485 to 1495. It now serves as a public hospital.

The façade is considered one of the masterpieces of the Renaissance style in Venice. The sculptures of *St. Mark* and members of the congregation and *Charity* are by Bartolomeo Bon, whereas the reliefs depicting the *Baptism and Healing of Anian* are by T. Lombardo. On the second floor is the **Salone del Capitolo** which has a fine 16th century wooden ceiling and an altar by followers of Sansovino. From here we enter the **Sala dell'Albergo** with a gold and blue painted wooden ceiling by Pietro and Biagio da Faenza. On the walls are paintings by Palma the Younger, Mansueti and Vittorio Belliniano. The bookcases contain texts from the Medical library.

From Campo Santi Giovanni e Paolo after going along the church's right flank, we go down the salizzada (paved lane) of the same name, then take the **Barbaria delle Tole**, the **Calle Caffettier,** crossing the **Campo Santa Giustina** and the canal of the same name. Here we turn left into the **Fondamenta Santa Giustina** and then right into the **Calle San Francesco** leading to the campo and church of the same name.

THE CHURCH OF SAN FRANCESCO DELLA VIGNA

The building itself was erected by Jacopo Sansovino in the 16th century, while the beautifully-proportioned façade, with its imposing portal flanked by four columns and crowned by a tympanum (gable), is an outstanding neo-Classical design by Palladio.

● THE INTERIOR

The interior is in the form of a Latin cross. Some noteworthy works of art are to be found inside the church. By the first altar in the transept is a rare painting by the 15th century painter, Antonio da Negroponte. This *Virgin Enthroned in Adoration* reveals the artist's lively imagination and delicate, harmonious style. In the chapel to the left of the choir are several fine sculptures by Pietro Lombardo and his followers. From the left transept we enter the **Holy Chapel** which contains a *Virgin and Saints* by Giovanni Bellini (1507). A *triptych* with *Sts. Jerome, Bernard,* and *Louis* by Antonio Vivarini is in the sacristy and a *Sacra Conversazione* painted by Veronese in 1551 is in the fifth chapel on the left.

To the right of the church we take the **Campo Confraternita** and, making a right cross the **Campo della Chiesa** and the **Rio San Francesco della Vigna.** We continue down the ramo (alley) of the same name which turns into the **Salizzada delle Gatte** up to the **Campo Foscolo** where we turn right into the **Calle Furlani.** Here we find the **Scuola di San Giorgio degli Schiavoni,** one of the most famous of the Venetian scuole, which was founded by a community of Dalmatians in the early 1500s. Inside, in the **Sala Terrena**, are superb painting cycles of the *Lives of Sts. George and Jerome* painted between 1502 and 1511 by one of Venice's foremost artists, Vittore Carpaccio. Of special note is the *St. George and the Dragon* which reveals the master's incredibly fertile imagination and lively style.

FIFTH ITINERARY

• •

THE RIVA DEGLI SCHIAVONI

A walk down the Riva degli Schiavoni from the Ponte della Paglia along the Canale di San Marco (St. Mark's Canal) to the Giardini di Castello (Castle Gardens) is one of the Venetians' favorites. The Riva was once the mooring station for trading vessels coming from Slavonic ports (present-day Dalmatia). Originally no wider than the Ponte della Paglia, it was paved in 1324 and then widened in 1780 by decree of the Senate. Running approximately a third of a mile, today it is a pleasant promenade filled with famous hotels and cafes.

Riva degli Schiavoni.

Just beyond the Ponte della Paglia is the stark façade of the **Prigioni Nuove** (New Prison) a neo-Classical building with a ground floor arcade; various architects such as Antonio Da Ponte, Rusconi, and Tommaso Contino had a hand in its construction between 1560 and 1614. Next is the **Palazzo Dandolo** with its lovely Gothic façade. Built in the 1400s, it changed owner- ship over the centuries (the Gritti, Bernardo, and Mocenigo families owned it at various times) until it was purchased by Sig. Danieli who restored it and turned it into one of the most luxurious hotels in the city. Crossing the **Ponte del Vin** and passing beneath a *"sottoportego"* (underpass), we come to the **Campo San Zaccaria** and the church of the same name.

This is one of the most interesting churches in Venice. Built in the 9th century, it was altered in the 15th and 16th centuries by Antonio Gambello and Mauro Coducci. Coducci also designed the distinctive six-section façade one of the foremost architectural designs to have come out of the Venetian Renaissance. The *statue of St. Zacharias* above the portal is by Alessandro Vittoria.

● THE INTERIOR

Interior of the church of San Zaccaria.

Lofty columns set off the three naves of this church which has a Gothic apse and peribolos with radiating chapels. The walls are hung with impressive paintings by the major late 17th century Venetian masters. At the second altar on the left is a famous altarpiece by Giovanni Bellini, the *Virgin and Child with Saints,* painted in 1505. From the right aisle we enter the **Chapel of St. Athanasius** which contains exquisite carved Gothic *choir stalls* (1455-1464), a *Virgin and Child* by Palma the Elder and, over the entrance, the *Birth of St. John the Baptist* by Tintoretto. From here we enter another chapel with a polygonal apse, the **Chapel of St. Tarsius**. A real gem, the chapel contains important ceiling frescoes representing *God the Father and Saints* painted in 1442 by the celebrated Florentine master Andrea del Castagno and, on the walls, three magnificent *altarpieces* by Giovanni d'Alemagna and Antonio Vivarini. At the end of the left aisle is the *tomb, with self-portrait of the sculptor Alessandro Vittoria,* who was buried here in 1605. Vittoria also left two exquisite *holy water fonts* in this same church.

Returning to the Riva degli Schiavoni, we cross the **Rio dei Greci** at the **Ponte di Pietà**, soon coming to the **church of Santa Maria della Pietà** which is a neo-classical building designed by Giorgio Massari in the mid-1700s. The plain yet elegant interior is elliptical in shape and adorned with a superb fresco representing the *Coronation of the Virgin* by Giovan Battista Tiepolo. Continuing on, we cross another little canal, making a left into the **Calle Dose** and proceed until we come to the **Campo Bandiera e Moro** where we find the church of San Giovanni in Bragora.

The façade of the church of San Zaccaria.

Although its origins date back to the 8th century, the church was completely rebuilt in 1475. The strange name "*Bragora*" could either be derived from agora, ancient Greek for square, or "*bragola*" (marketplace) in Venetian dialect. The façade is one of the finest examples of the late Venetian Gothic style.

● THE INTERIOR

It has single aisles and a Gothic-style beamed ceiling. Over the entrance, *Christ before Caiaphas* by Palma the Younger. On the nave walls and the triumphal arch, are an *Annunciation,* saints, and other 15th century frescoes by a provincial artist, Tommaso di Zorzi. In the second chapel of the right aisle, an *altarpiece with St. John the Beggar,* and, in the lunette, the *Removal of the Body of St. John to Venice* by Jacopo Marieschi (the mortal remains of the saint are in an urn beneath the altar). At the end of the right aisle over the sacristy door is a painting of *Christ Blessing* by Alvise Vivarini (1493). The Renaissance *choir* was built by Sebastiano Mariani between 1485 and 1488. On the pillars by the entrance are two works by Vivarini, *St. Helen and Constantine by the Cross* on the right and *Christ Resurrected* on the left. On the main altar are three sculptures: *Faith* by Antonio Gai, *St. John the Evangelist,* and *St. John the Beggar* by Giovanni Marchiori. In the apse is a fine *Baptism of Christ* by Cima da Conegliano. On the walls are the *Last Supper* by Paris Bordone and the *Washing of the Feet* by Palma the Younger. In the left aisle, in the chapel closest to the choir, are two noteworthy altarpieces: a triptych representing the *Virgin Between Sts. Andrew and John the Baptist*, by Bartolomeo Vivarini on the right and *Sts. Andrew, Jerome,* and *Martin* on the left.

We return to the Riva degli Schiavoni and, after crossing another picturesque canal, the **Rio della Ca' di Dio**, which turns into the **Riva della Ca' di Dio**, we take the **Riva San Biagio**. Following the **Rio dell'Arsenale** we soon come to the **Arsenal** which was supposedly founded by Doge Ardelaffo Falier in the early 12th century. Built as a shipyard for the Republic's fleet, it underwent alterations and enlargements throughout the centuries. The impressive entrance consists of a gateway flanked by two marble *lions,* which were carried off as booty by doge and admiral Francesco Morosini. One of the 16th century buildings that once belonged to the old Arsenal presently houses the **Museo Storico Navale** (the Museum of Naval History) which contains relics of Venice's glorious seafaring past. One of the oustanding models of seacraft on display is certainly the *Bucintoro,* a faithful 19th century reproduction of the original built in 1728. This

The Arsenal.

craft was traditionally used by the doges for their periodic Marriage to the Sea ceremonies. In addition, the museum collection includes many kinds of weapons, portraits of doges and admirals, as well as relics and models of craft used in the two world wars. The Riva di San Biagio runs into the **Riva dei Sette Martiri** which leads us to the **Giardini Pubblici di Castello** (the Castle Park) designed by Antonio Selva at the beginning of the 19th century on a commission from Napoleon Bonaparte. Every other year this is the site of the world-famous **International Exhibition of Modern Art** which, from 1895, has drawn the participation of renowned artists from every corner of the globe. Continuing along the **Via Garibaldi** by the park entrance and along the **Fondamenta Sant'Anna,** we come to a bridge which we cross to reach the **Isola di San Pietro**, a picturesque island of fishermen's houses, and the church of the same name.

The church was built in the 8th century on the site of an even older sanctuary, and then remodeled over the centuries. It served as Venice's cathedral until the early 1900s. Its present-day appearance is the achievement of a late 16th century architect, Francesco Smeraldi, who based the façade on a design by Palladio, and, in fact, it bears the great architect's hallmark: a huge portal with a pair of columns on either side topped by a tympanum. The belfry leaning considerably to one side recalls the famous tower of Pisa.

● THE INTERIOR

The domed church was rebuilt in the first half of 17th century. One of the most interesting works of art contained inside is the so-called *Cattedra di Pietro* (Peter's Throne) standing in the right aisle. According to tradition, the cattedra, built in the 13th century from older pieces of Islamic art, was used by St. Peter in Antioch. The *main altar* designed by Baldassarre Longhena in the mid-1600s contains the *mortal remains of St. Lorenzo Giustiniani*, the first patriarch of Venice. Along the choir walls are paintings by various artists depicting scenes from the life of the saint. Longhena is also responsible for the fine **Vendramin Chapel** with an elaborate Baroque decorative scheme and a *Virgin and Child* by Luca Giordano on the altar. From the left aisle we enter the late Gothic **Lando Chapel** built in the 15th century.

SIXTH ITINERARY

• •

O ur itinerary starts out from the **Campo San Bartolomeo** which we recommend reaching by way of the Mercerie from Piazza San Marco. In the middle of the bustling square is the *monument to Carlo Goldoni.* the great 18th century Venetian playwright whose plays so wonderfully reflect the Venetian spirit of his day. On one side of the square, is the **church of San Bartolomeo,** originally built in the 12th century, but rebuilt in the 1700s. The Baroque belltower was erected in 1747 by Scalfarotto. The single-aisled domed church contains works by Sebastiano del Piombo and Palma the Younger. From the Campo di San Bartolomeo we soon reach the **Rialto Bridge** with its picturesque shops and marvelous view over the Grand Canal. If, on the other hand, we go along the Fondaco dei Tedeschi, we come to the salizzada and church of San Giovanni Crisostomo.

Two views of the inside of the Rialto Bridge.

THE CHURCH OF SAN GIOVANNI CRISOSTOMO

O nce this church looked out on the Grand Canal, although after being gutted in a fire in 1475, it was rebuilt between 1497 and 1504 by Mauro Coducci on its present location. The façade with its curvilinear design is extremely elegant. The belltower was built in the 1500s.

● THE INTERIOR

The church is in the shape of a Greek cross, with barrel vaults and a dome at the transept. The first altar on the right is adorned with a late work by Giovanni Bellini, *Sts. Christopher, Jerome, and* *Augustine.* On either side of the altar are *organ panels* painted by Giovanni Mansueti. On the main altar is a celebrated *altarpiece* by Sebastiano del Piombo showing *St. Chrysostomos and Other Saints,* painted in the early 1500s.

133

We continue along the **Salizzada San Giovanni Crisostomo** to the **Campiello Corner**. Then right into the **Salizzada San Canciano** which leads into the **Campiello Santa Maria Nova** with the church of Santa Maria dei Miracoli.

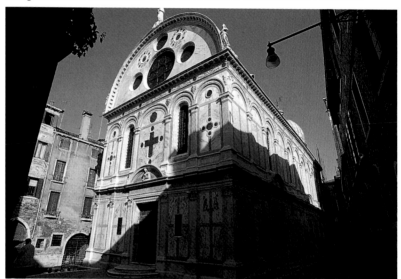

 # THE CHURCH OF SANTA MARIA DEI MIRACOLI

Pietro Lombardo designed this Renaissance church in 1481. Its unusual and very attractive façade sports marble decoration over the two storey central portal surmounted by two huge windows.

● THE INTERIOR

The walls of the rectangular church are lined in precious marble and the coffered ceiling is divided into 50 lacunars with heads of *Prophets* and *Saints* by Pier Maria Pennacchi (1528). The raised *choir*, a masterpiece of decorative art created by the Lombardo brothers, is reached by an elegant staircase. The main altar is surmounted by a dome.

Returning to the Campiello Corner, we turn right and, crossing the **Rio Santi Apostoli**, we reach the campo and church of the same name.

 # THE CHURCH OF SANTI APOSTOLI

This church's origins date from long ago, although it was remodeled several times until 1575 when it was radically restructured to its present form. On the Campo di Santi Apostoli is a house oddly nestled in between the belltower and the dome of the Corner Chapel. The belltower of 1672 was completed with a bellchamber designed by Andrea Tirali. The brick façade is not particularly noteworthy.

134

● THE INTERIOR

Inside the rectangular church, we first note the ceiling with frescoes of the *Glorification of the Eucharist* and the *Apostles* by Fabio Canal and G. Gaspari (1748). The **Cappella Corner** on the right side was remodeled in the 16th century; its Lombard-style architecture has been attributed to Mauro Coducci. On the right wall is the *tomb of Marco Corner* attributed to Tullio Lombardo, the one on the left is the *tomb of Cardinal Giorgio Corner.* On the altar is a fine *altarpiece* depicting the *Communion of St. Lucy* by Giovan Battista Tiepolo and, on the altar of the next chapel, a painting of the *Nativity of the Virgin* by Giorgio Contarini. In another of the righthand chapels we can see the remains of Byzantine frescoes showing the *Deposition from the Cross* and the *Burial of Christ.* Nearby is a relief depicting *St. Sebastian,* a 16th century work by Tullio Lombardo. In the choir, on the right, is a *Last Supper* by Cesare da Conegliano (16th century) and, on the left the *Shower of Manna* by followers of Paolo Veronese.

Going left, facing the church, we take the **Calle Pistor** until we reach the **Rio Terrà Franceschi** where we turn first right then left along the **Rio Terrà Santi Apostoli.** After crossing the **Rio Terrà Barba Fruttarol** we go down the **Calle Spezier** and the **Salizzada Seriman** which, by way of the **Rio Santa Caterina** leads to the peaceful **Campo dei Gesuiti** and the church of the same name. This, in fact, is one of the loveliest spots in Venice - not even the dynamic sculpture on the church façade can take away from the square's overall relaxing effect.

✝ THE CHURCH DEI GESUITI (Jesuits)

Although this grandiose church was established in the 12th century for the Order of the Cross-Bearers it was turned over to the Jesuits in 1656 and remodeled by Domenico Rossi between 1715 and 1730. The imposing Baroque façade designed by Fattoretto is adorned with statues of the 12 *Apostles* (by F. Penso, the Groppelli brothers, and P. Baratta). There is also a fine portal with *Angels* by Matteo Calderoni and, in the tympanum, the *Assumption of the Virgin* by G. Torretto.

Right: *the church dei Gesuiti.*
Preceding page: *the church of Santa Maria dei Miracoli.*

● THE INTERIOR

The church has a Latin-cross plan and is wholly decorated with striking patterns of colored marble inlay. The stucco ceiling is by A. Stazio and the frescoes by Fontebasso. On the wall by the entrance is a *monument* by G. B. Longhena and a *bust of Priamo Da Lezze* by Jacopo Sansovino. On the first altar on the right, the *Guardian Angel* by Palma the Younger, in the second, a *statue of St. Barbara* by Morlaiter. and in the third, *Virgin and Saints* by Balestra. In the right transept is a *statue of St. Ignatius* by P. Baratta. In the chapel to the right of the main chapel is *St. Francis Xavier Preaching* by P. Liberi. The choir has elaborate architecture influenced by the style of Bernini by Father G. Pozzo, sculptures by Toretto, and frescoes by L. Dorigny. Two outstanding paintings are hanging here: the *Assumption of the Virgin* by Jacopo Tintoretto and the *Martyrdom of St. Lawrence* by Titian. In the sacristy is a painting cycle on the theme of the Order of the Cross Bearers executed by Palma the Younger between 1589 and 1593.

From the Campo dei Gesuiti we follow the **Rio Santa Caterina**. Practically at the end, we cross to the other side and go left along the **Calle Racchetta** and then take the **Calle Priuli** until reaching the **Strada Nuova.** We follow the Strada Nuova on the left side for just a short way until we come, on the right, to the **Ca' d'Oro**, inside of which is the Franchetti Gallery.

 # THE FRANCHETTI GALLERY

The palace, along with its furnishings and an extensive collection of paintings of various periods and schools, was donated to the Italian state by Baron Giorgio Franchetti in 1916 and opened to the public in 1927. Nevertheless, none of works or rooms bear identification plates or labels in accordance with Baron Franchetti's wish that it retain the appearance of a collection in a private home rather than take on the anonymous look of a state museum.

We shall list only the most significant of the many important works in the collection. In order to make it easier for you to see the gallery, we have numbers for the rooms which, as was previously mentioned, have deliberately been kept "unidentified". In the center of the splendid arcaded courtyard adorned with Roman and Greek sculpture is a fine 15th century marble well-curb. By the brick wall, a staircase resting on pointed arches leads up to the second floor loggia, or gallery, along which tapestries and sculpture are displayed. In the first room are two works by Carpaccio, the *Annunciation* and the *Death of the Virgin,* originally from the Scuola degli Albanesi, and an *altar-piece* with the *Passion of Christ* by Antonio Vivarini. In the second room is a *Sleeping Venus* by Paris Bordone. In the third, a *bust of Benedetto Manzini* by Vittoria. The fourth room contains one of the museum's finest works, *Venus at Her Mirror* by Titian. Another masterpiece hangs in the sixth room, *St. Sebastian* by Mantegna. In the seventh room on the third floor is a handsome *Portrait of a Gentleman* by Van Dyck. In the ninth room the two outstanding works are Pontormo's *Portrait of a Girl* and Filippo Lippi's *Nativity.*

Right: **Allegory of Wealth,** *Florentine school* (XVI cent.).
Preceding page: **View of the Wharf and Punta della Dogana,** by *Francesco Guardi*

Among the many fine works in the tenth room we shall mention two lovely *landscapes* by Francesco Guardi, the *Flagellation* by Luca Signorelli and a noteworthy 15th century *Crucifixion* attributed to Jan Van Eyck. In the eleventh room are several Tintoretto *portraits* and other masterpieces of 16th century painting. From the third floor we may enter the remaining rooms of the gallery, which are actually part of the adjoining Palazzo Giusti; three of them contain Venetian school bronzes and Dutch and Flemish paintings.

After leaving the Franchetti Gallery, we go left down the Strada Nuova, cross the **Rio di Noale** and take the **Strada Nuova Santa Fosca** which leads to the campo of the same name. After crossing the **Rio Santa Fosca** we proceed along the **Calle Zancani** until **Campo San Marzial**. Passing the Baroque **church of San Marzial**, we go on and cross the **Rio della Misericordia** and turn left into the fondamenta of the same name until we reach **Calle Larga** which we take to cross the **Rio della Sensa** and then the **Rio della Madonna dell'Orto**. We are now in the campo of the same name, in front of the church of the Madonna dell'Orto.

 # THE CHURCH OF MADONNA DELL' ORTO

According to an old tradition, a miraculous statue of the *Virgin* (today preserved inside the Church) was found in the orto (garden) which originally covered this zone. The façade is an attractive mixture ot the Romanesque and Gothic styles. The *statues of the Apostles* in the upper niches of the sides of the façade are by followers of the Dalle Masegnes.

● **THE INTERIOR**

The interior is built on a basilica plan; the aisles are offset by ten marble columns and a polygonal apse. The church contains numerous paintings by Jacopo Robusti, better known as Tintoretto, who was buried here in 1594. His tomb, marked by a simple stone plaque, is inside the church to the right of the choir. By the first altar of the right aisle is *St. John in Ecstasy with Other Saints,* the masterpiece of Cima da Conegliano (1493). Above the **Chapel of St. Maurus** is Tintoretto's *Presentation of the Virgin at the Temple.* The paintings in the choir (the *Last Judgement, Adoration of the Golden Calf,* and *Moses Receiving the Tablets of the Law*) are all by Titian who painted them when he had reached the height of his creative powers. In the fourth chapel off the left aisle is another Tintoretto, *St. Agnes Raising Licino from the Dead.* The *Virgin and Child* in the first chapel is by Giovanni Bellini.

Two views of the Canale di Cannaregio.

Proceeding along the **Fondamenta della Madonna dell'Orto**, we cross the canal on the left side arriving at the **Fondamenta della Sensa** where we turn right and walk along the canal and cross it at the **Ponte della Malvasia**. Going down the calle of the same name, we cross the **Rio della Misericordia** and take the **Calle degli Ormesini** which leads to the **Rio Terrà Farsetti**, and, on the right, to the **Rio Terrà San Leonardo** which encircle the fascinating **Jewish ghetto** with its old buildings and synagogues. Having thus arrived at the **Canale di**

The market of the Ponte delle Guglie.

Right: *The Canale di Cannaregio flows into the Grand Canal*; below: *detail of the gate of Palazzo Labia.*

Cannaregio the second largest waterway in Venice after the Grand Canal, we are in the heart of one of the most picturesque neighborhoods in Venice. We cross the Cannaregio at the **Ponte delle Guglie**, a 16th century bridge rebuilt in the 1700s and characterized by obelisks on either end. Just beyond the bridge is the 18th century **Palazzo Labia** whose interior is adorned with frescoes by Tiepolo. Next comes the **church of San Geremia** on the campo of the same name. Although the church was originally built in the 13th century, its present appearance dates from the 1700s when its first façade was built (the other was erected 19th century). The bell-tower, on the other hand retains its original 13th century appearance. Inside the Greek cross-shaped buildings are *relics of St. Lucy*.

Along the **Lista di Spagna** we reach the church of the Scalzi.

139

THE CHURCH OF SANTA MARIA DI NAZARETH
(or DEGLI SCALZI)

Baldassarre Longhena was commissioned by the Barefoot (scalzi) Carmelite monks to design the church in 1670, but it was not finished until 1705, the year it was also consecrated. The façade, an outstanding example of the Venetian Baroque, was designed by Giuseppe Sardi, who drew his inspiration from Classical architecture. It consists of two tiers of twin columns framing huge niches which contain statues presumably carved by Bernardino Falcone. The whole is surmounted by a triangular tympanum adorned with sculpture. Unfortunately, one of the church's prize artworks, a fresco portraying the *Transportation from the House of Loreto*, by Giovan Battista Tiepolo, was destroyed during World War I. It has since been replaced by another fresco, the *Proclamation of the Motherhood of the Virgin at the Council of Ephesus*, by the painter Ettore Tito.

The interior of the church of Santa Maria di Nazareth.
Preceding page: *the church of Santa Maria di Nazareth.*

● THE INTERIOR

The elaborate decoration of the interior perfectly reflects the rich decoration of the exterior. The inside is a profusion of sculpture, gilded stucco and colored marble. The main altar, crowned by a canopy resting on eight marble columns, was designed by Giuseppe Pozzo in the exuberant Baroque style of the day. The *statues of St. Theresa* and *St. John of the Cross* on either side of the altar are fine works attributed to Bernardino Falcone. In the second chapel on the right is a ceiling fresco by Giovan Battista Tiepolo depicting *St. Theresa in Glory*. Another Tiepolo ceiling fresco is to be found in the first chapel on the left. It represents the *Sermon in the Garden* and the *Angel of the Passion*. In the second chapel on the left known as the **Chapel of St. Carmel**, is the *tomb of Ludovico Manin*, the last doge of the Serenissima Repubblica di San Marco who ceased being such on May 12, 1797 when the French overthrew the Republic.

We return to the Cannaregio Canal and turn left into the **Fondamenta Venier** and continue, passing the **Fondamenta Savorgan**, until we come to the **Fondamenta di San Giobbe** and the church of the same name.

Construction of the church lasted through second half of the 15th century. The architects Antonio Gambello, Pietro Lombardo; and Guglielmo Bergamasco all had a hand in it. The finely-crafted portal adorned with *statues of St. Bernardino, St. Anthony,* and *St. Louis* was created by Bergamasco.

● THE INTERIOR

At the far end of the church are the entrances to the **Contarini Chapel,** which contains a charming *Nativity* by Savolto, and the Renaissance sacristy. From the sacristy we enter the **Da Mula Chapel** adorned with a *triptych* by Antonio Vivarini. The fine choir is decorated with sculpture by Pietro Lombardo and helpers. The second chapel on the left has a glazed terracotta ceiling decoration by the Della Robbias.

The church of San Giobbe.

SEVENTH ITINERARY

The church of San Giacomo di Rialto.

T his itinerary starts out from the Rialto Bridge. Taking the bustling **Ruga degli Orefici**, undoubtedly one of the most picturesque spots in Venice with its colorful cluster of fruit and vegetable stands. We immediately come to the **church of San Giacomo di Rialto** on our right which, according to tradition, is the oldest church in the city. However, despite the fact that the building does actually date back to the 11th century, it underwent extensive remodeling in the 1600s. The façade is preceded by a 15th century porch and has a giant clock over the center window. Inside are works by Marco Vecellio and Leandro Bassano. A bit farther on, we turn into the **Ruga Vecchia San Zuane** and proceed until we reach the church of San Giovanni Elemosinario.

THE CHURCH OF SAN GIOVANNI ELEMOSINARIO

O riginally built in 1071, it was gutted in a fire in 1513 and reconstructed by Scarpagnino in 1530. The belltower, which emerged unscathed, is the original one put up between 1398 and 1410.

● THE INTERIOR

The interior in the shape of a Greek cross is covered with a dome. On the entrance wall is a *Crucifixion* by L. Corona who also painted the *Shower of Manna* on the right wall. In the chapel to the right of the main one is a fine painting by Pordenone depicting *St. Sebastian, St. Catherine,* and *St. Roch.* In the sacristy the ceiling fresco of *St. Augustine* and the *Virgin and St. Philip* on the altar are by G. V. Pittoni. In the choir by the main altar is a masterpiece painted by Titian in 1545, *St. John the Beggar.* In the lunette there is the *Resurrection* by L. Corona and, on the walls, two other works by the same artist representing the *Sermon in the Garden* and the *Crucifixion.* The *Last*

143

Supper on the left is by Aliense. On the left wall of the church is *Constantine with the Cross* by Palma the Younger and, on the door beside, are three panel paintings by Marco Vercellio. They represent *St. John the Beggar, Doge Donato Visiting the Church,* and *St. Mark.*

Rio delle Beccarie.

Returning to the Ruga degli Orefici, we turn left into the **Ruga degli Speziali** which comes out into the **Campo delle Beccarie.** On the right is the fascinating loggia del Mercato del Pesce or **Pescheria** (Fish Market). After crossing the **Rio delle Beccarie** and the **Calle dei Botterie**, we come out in the **Calle Campanile** and, keeping left, we proceed to the campo on which stands the ancient **church of San Cassiano** rebuilt, however, in the 17th century. Inside are several famous Tintorettos, including a superb *Crucifixion.* After crossing the **Rio San Cassiano**, we go right along the **Calle della Regina,** then left along the **Calle Tiossi,** until, passing the **Rio delle Due Torri,** we reach the **Fondamenta Pesaro** and the palace of the same name. In the Palazzo Pesaro are two museums, the Gallery of Modern Art and the Oriental Art Museum.

🏛 THE INTERNATIONAL GALLERY OF MODERN ART

Palazzo Pesaro, *home of the Gallery of Modern Art and the Oriental Museum.*

Founded in 1897, the collection has been steadily expanded as works from the famous Venice Biennial Art Exhibition have been added to it. The paintings and sculptures displayed range from the 19th and 20th century Venetian schools to a remarkable group of Italian and non-Italian contemporary masters.

Among the many noteworthy artists we shall cite just a handful: Medardo Rosso (the *Concierge,* the *Laughing Lady,* Mrs. *Noble)* Giorgio Morandi, Zandomeneghi, Arturo Martini, Manzu (the *Great Cardinal),* Emilio Greco (*Head of a Lady)*, Francesco Hayez (*Self-portrait)*, Telemaco Signorini (*November)*, Giovanni Fattori, Auguste Rodin (the *Age of Bronze)*, Kandinsky, Klee, Klimt (*Salome)* Henry Moore, Savinio, De Chirico, De Pisis and a host of others.

THE ORIENTAL MUSEUM

The museum was set up in 1928 starting out with the collection donated by Count Enrico Bardi di Bardone. The only one of its kind on the Italian peninsula, it contains art works and artifacts from all over Asia.

The collection includes many fine pieces. There are Chinese and Japanese weapons and armor, both for parade and military use, a series of exquisite 17th and 18th century painted screens from Japan, delicate Chinese porcelain, painted fabrics from Thailand and Java, a superb Khmer statue of a smiling *Bodhisatva* (Buddhist saint) carved out of basalt from Cambodia, as well as costumes and ritual masks from various countries, Japanese lacquered pieces and objects of everyday use ranging from combs, trinkets, and artifacts to the incredible kosseu (embroidered garments made in China). Periodically important international art exhibitions are held in the Palazzo Pesaro.

From Palazzo Pesaro we cross the **Rio della Pergola** at the **Ponte Pesaro** and then the **Rio San Stae**, reaching, on the right, the **church of San Stae** which overlooks the Grand Canal ("*Stae*" in Venetian dialect means Eustache and, in fact, the church is dedicated to St. Eustache). The church, built in the early 18th century by Domenico Rossi, is a fine example of the Baroque style. The façade with great columns surmounted by a tympanum is adorned with a profusion of sculpture. Inside are the *Martyrdom of St. Bartholomew*, a youthful work by Tiepolo and a *Martyrdom of St. James* by Piazzetta. Alongside the church we can see the façade of the **Scuola dei Battiloro e Tiraoro**.

We continue along the **Salizzada San Stae**; then, after crossing the **Rio del Megio**, we turn right into the **Calle Tintor**. On the left we soon come to the **Campo San Giacomo dell'Orio** and church of the same name which rises on an attractive square perenially alive with the excited chatter of children at play.

The church of San Stae.

THE CHURCH OF SAN GIACOMO DELL'ORIO

Although the church's origins go far back, it was extensively remodeled in the Renaissance period and restored in 1909. The Romanesque belltower, pierced by graceful mullioned windows dates from the 1200s. The interior is in the shape of a Latin cross and has a beamed ceiling. The new sacristy (entered from the right transept) contains a ceiling frescoed by Veronese with *Allegories of Faith*. Paintings by Veronese, Francesco Bassano, and Giovanni Buonconsiglio, known as Marescalco, hang on the walls. In the choir is a *Virgin and Child with Saints* by Lorenzo Lotto.

The church of San Giacomo dell'Orio on the campo of the same name.

A door to the left of the main chapel leads to the old sacristy adorned with paintings by Palma the Younger (1575).

We cross the square and, reaching the **Rio di San Giacomo**, we cross it. Then we take the sottoportego coming out on the **Corte dell'Anatomia**, just as lonely and quiet as Campo San Giacomo was full of life. To the left, a low underpass leads to the **Campiello delle Strope** which we cross, and then we turn left into the **Calle del Cristo**, passing a bridge, and turn left again following the canal. Immediately we turn right into the **Calle del Cafetier** and, after a brief stretch, we reach the Scuola Grande di San Giovanni Evangelista on the right.

THE SCUOLA DI SAN GIOVANNI EVANGELISTA

The Scuola was founded as pilgrims' lodgings in 1261. Then, in 1340, it became headquarters for the Confraternity of the Battuti whose patron saint was St. John the Evangelist. The building, a masterpiece of the Venetian Renaissance style, dates from 1454. The courtyard was designed by Pietro Lombardo in 1481 while Mauro Coducci designed the superb portal and main hall in 1512. The upper floor is mostly occupied by a great hall which contains an impressive *altar* (built by G. Massari in 1730), who also remodeled Coducci's design of the room according to 18th century taste. On the altar is a *statue of St. John* by Morlaiter and stories from the lives of various saints by Marieschi and Guarana. On the ceiling is the *Struggle between Christ and the Antichrist* by G. Angeli, while the figures on the sides are by G. Diziani. The other paintings by the altar are *St. John* by Marieschi, the *Seven Angels* and *Seven Vases* in octagonal frames opposite by J. Guarana, and the *Scenes from the Apocalypse* by Domenico Tiepolo. On the walls of the right of the door are two paintings by Domenico Tintoretto, the *Transfiguration* and *Fall of the Temple*. In the **Sala della Croce**, with a ceiling fresco of *Triumph of the Cross* by F. Maggiotto, is an exquisite urn, the *Reliquary of the Cross*. The four *stories of the Apocalypse* on the walls of the **Sala dell'Albergo** are by Palma the Younger, while the frescoed ceiling of the **Saletta dell'Archivio** is by Guarana.

We continue along the **Calle Magazzen**, then turn left into **Rio Terrà San Toma**. Proceeding, on the right, we cross the **Ponte San Stin**, taking the **Fondamenta dei Frari** where we immediately turn right and soon reach the **Campo dei Frari**.

Below, from the left: *Scuola di San Giovanni Evangelista,* and *the "campiello" of the same name.*

This Romanesque-Gothic style Franciscan church, like its Dominican counterpart San Zanipolo, contains the tombs of a number of famous Venetians. Begun by the Franciscan monks in 1250, after a design attributed to Nicola Pisano, it was later re-elaborated and enlarged by Scipione Bon in 1338, though it was not finished until 1443. The unadorned façade is divided into three sections by pilaster strips surmounted by pinnacles. The statues over the central portal are by Alessandro Vittoria (1581). The Romanesque belltower is the second tallest in Venice, right after St. Mark's.

Church of Santa Maria Gloriosa dei Frari.

The interior of the church of Santa Maria Gloriosa dei Frari.

● THE INTERIOR

The Latin cross interior, with aisles set off by twelve plain columns, is truly majestic in its Franciscan simplicity. The church contains funerary monuments of numerous famous Venetians of the 14th to 18th centuries, not the least of which is Titian's. Right aisle: the first altar by Longhena has sculpture by Giusto le Court, second bay, the *tomb of Titian,* who died of plague in 1576, is a mediocre work executed by followers of Canova in 1852; third altar, sculptures by Alessandro Vittoria, among which a fine *St. Jerome.* To the right of the righthand transept is the *monument to Jacopo Marcello,* the Venetian admiral, by Pietro Lombardo. In the sacristy which looks like a beautiful miniature church is a masterpiece by Giovanni Bellini, still in its original frame, on the altar. The *triptych* painted in 1488 depicts the *Virgin Enthroned, Music-making Angels,* and *Saints.* In the third apse chapel is another triptych this one by Bartolomeo Vivarini. On the altar of the first chapel is a *statue of St. John the Baptist* by Donatello. The choir: on the right wall is the Gothic-

Renaissance *monument to Doge Francesco Foscari* by the Bregno brothers (c. 1475). On the left wall, a Renaissance masterpiece, the *monument to Doge Nicolò Tron* by Antonio Rizzo (1476). Behind the main altar is Titian's celebrated altarpiece, the *Assumption of the Virgin* of 1518, regarded as one of the greatest compositional feats in art. In the first apse chapel on the left is a fine altarpiece by Bernardo Licinio (1535); in the third one, an altarpiece by Alvise Vivarini and Marco Basaiti representing *St. Ambrose Enthroned* (1503). In the fourth chapel is a *triptych* by Bartolomeo Vivarini on the altar and, on the baptismal font, a *statue of St. John the Baptist* by Sansovino (1554). Left aisle: over the second altar, another masterpiece by Titian, the *Pesaro Altarpiece*, depicting the *Virgin with Members of the Pesaro Family*, painted by the master in 1526. Farther on is a huge *monument to Doge Giovanni Pesaro* by Longhena (1669), followed by the *tomb of Antonio Canova* built from a design left by the great sculptor himself.

Walking along the left side of the church and around its rear apses, we reach the **Campo San Rocco** with its famous scuola and church of the same name.

THE SCUOLA GRANDE DI SAN ROCCO (School of St. Roch)

Bartolomeo Bon the Younger, commissioned by the Confraternity of St. Roch, began work on the building in 1517. The project was continued by Sante Lombardo and finally completed by Antonio Scarpagnino in 1549. This is the most famous of the numerous Venetian scuole, mainly due to the presence of the great cycle of paintings by Jacopo Tintoretto inside.

Scuola Grande di San Rocco;
below: *the courtyard.*

In order to follow the great painting cycles in chronological order, we cross the main hall on the ground floor (which we shall visit on the way back) and go to the second floor, where we enter the **Sala dell 'Albergo**, which Tintoretto began decorating in 1564. On the ceiling, *St. Roch in Glory*, on the wall, the grandiose *Crucifixion* and around the room, starting on the right, the *Calvary of Christ* two figures of *Prophets, Christ before Pilate,* and *Christ*

Crowned with Thorns. The *Christ Carrying the Cross* on the easel has been variously attributed to Giorgione and Titian. We now enter the huge main hall. To the left of the door is a *self-portrait* of Tintoretto at the age of 66. On the gilded carved ceiling divided into compartments are 21 paintings by Tintoretto. The best vantage point is from the middle of the side opposite the altar. The subjects of the paintings are: *Adam and Eve, Moses Causing Water to Flow from the Rock*; on the left, *God Appearing to Moses*; on the right *Crossing of the Red Sea, Jonah Coming Out of the Whale*, the *Plague of Snakes;* on the left, *Ezechiel's Vision*; on the right, *Jacob's Ladder*, the *Sacrifice of Isaac,* the *Shower of Manna*; on the left, *Elijah and the Angel*; on the right, *Elisha Distributing Bread,* and the *Jewish Passover*. On the altar is *St. Roch in Glory Flanked by the Annunciation* by Titian and the *Visitation* by Tintoretto. Returning to the far wall, from left to right we see: *St. Roch, St. Sebastian,* the *Nativity*, the *Baptism of Christ*, the *Resurrection*, the *Sermon in the Garden*, the *Last Supper;* then crossing the room in front of the altar, the *Multiplication of the Loaves,* the *Resurrection of Lazarus,* the *Ascension*, the *Healing of the Cripple,* and *Christ and Satan*. By the altar is the entrance to the **Sala della Cancelleria** which contains an *Ecce Homo* attributed to Titian, a *St. Roch* by Bernardo Strozzi and a *St. Roch in Glory* by C. Angeli. We now retrace our steps, going down the monumental staircase adorned with two huge 17th century paintings by A. Zanchi and Pietro Negri, and enter the ground floor hall. The spatial effect of the double row of Corinthian columns running the length of the room is quite striking. On the walls are eight massive paintings by Tintoretto dating from 1583 to 1587. Starting on the left, their subjects are: the *Annunciation,* the *Adoration of the Magi,* the *Flight into Egypt,* the *Slaughter of the Innocents, St. Mary Magdalene,* the *Circumcision,* and the *Assumption of the Virgin.*

 # THE CHURCH OF SAN ROCCO

Originally a Renaissance building, the church was rebuilt in the 18th century by Scalfarotto, although the façade is by Bernardo Maccaruzzi. The interior, with a dome at the choir crossing, contains a series of paintings by Tintoretto. To the right of the organ, the *Annunciation,* to the left, *St. Roch Presented to the Pope* and above the first altar on the right, *St. Roch in the Desert*. The story of St. Roch is continued along the walls of the choir.

From the Campo San Rocco, we continue along the **Calle Larga Prima** which leads into the Campo San Tomà. Here we find the **Scuola dei Calegheri**, which once belonged to a congregation of shoemakers, and which has a relief over the portal showing *St. Mark Healing the Shoemaker Aniano* (attributed to Pietro Lombardo). Crossing the **Rio San Tomà** on the left after crossing the campo, we enter the **Calle dei Nomboli** and, on the left, the street of the same name, then make a right into the **Calle dei Saoneri.** We cross the **Rio di San Polo** and, by way of the salizzada we reach the **Campo di San Polo.** This is the largest campo in Venice, the site of festivals, games and every sort of public event. The church on the square is dedicated to St. Paul (San Polo, in dialect).

Campo San Polo.

✝ THE CHURCH OF SAN POLO

According to tradition the church was founded in 837 by Doge Pietro Gradonico. It was then rebuilt in the Gothic style and remodeled many times throughout the centuries. Its lovely belltower dates from 1362.

● THE INTERIOR

It is in the form of a basilica with single aisles. On the inside façade are two fine works, the *Communion of the Apostles* by Jacopo Tintoretto and the *Baptism of Constantine* by Piazza. Over the first altar on the right is the *Assumption of the Virgin* by Jacopo Tintoretto. In the **Chapel of the Blessed Sacrament** built in the Lombard style are four paintings by Giuseppe Salviati recounting *Episodes from the Life of Christ.* In the choir are paintings by Palma the Younger whose subjects are: the *Temptation and Liberation of St. Anthony*, the *Conversion of St. Paul*, the *Giving of the Keys to St. Peter,* and *St. Mark Preaching.* In addition, there are two paintings by G. B. Tiepolo representing *Angels in Glory* and the *Via Crucis.* On the main altar, between bronze *statues of St. Paul and St. Anthony Abbot* by Vittoria, is a 15th century painted *Crucifix.* The chapel to the left of the main chapel contains a *Visitation* by Veronese. At the second altar on the left is the *Virgin with St. John Nepomucenus* by G. B. Tiepolo.

EIGHTH ITINERARY

• •

Passing the Gothic **Palazzo Soranzo**, we cross the **Rio della Madonnetta** by way of the **Calle Cavalli**, then, to the left, we take the **Rio di Sant'Aponal** and again cross it on the right by the 16th century **Casa di Bianca Cappello** (House of Bianca Cappello). Continuing along the **Rio Terrà Sant'Aponal** we reach the **church of Sant'Aponal** (St. Apollinare). The *Crucifixion* and other *Scenes from the Life of Christ* on the portal date from 1294, although the façade was remodeled in the 15th century. The building itself was built in the Gothic style. The interior is adorned with Renaissance altars. On the main altar is the *Martyrdom of St. Apollinare* by L. Querena. 18th and 19th century canvases decorate the other altars, while the sculpture dates from various periods.

This itinerary starts out from Piazza San Marco, passing beneath the arcade of the Napoleonic Wing on the side opposite the church. After going down the **Calle dell'Ascension**, we take the salizzada leading to the campo and church of San Moise.

The church of San Moisè.

THE CHURCH OF SAN MOISE

There has been a church on this spot since the 8th century A.D. In the 10th century the original structure was rebuilt by a certain Moise Venier who dedicated it to his own name-saint, St. Moise. Later, in the 14th century, the lovely belltower with its distinctive brick spire was raised alongside it. The Baroque façade was designed in the second half of the 17th century by Alessandro Tremignon for Vincenzo Fini whose bust can be seen on the obelisk above the central portal (although Tremignon commissioned the sculptor Enrico Meyring with the actual execution of the decorative scheme). Many of the sculptures had to be removed during the 19th century, since they were in danger of toppling, which means that the decoration which today appears exaggeratedly ornate, was even more so in the original version.

● THE INTERIOR

The ceiling of the church is frescoed with the *Vision of Moses* by Niccolo Bambini. The first altar on the right is adorned with an 18th century marble *Pietà* by Antonio Corradini and a painting in the Caraccis' style representing the *Adoration of the Magi* by Giuseppe Diamantini. Also on the right is a fine pulpit carved in the 18th century by Tagliapietra. In the second altar is the *Invention of the Cross* by Pietro Liberi.

In the sacristy is a bronze altar frontal with a *Deposition* scene, by the 17th century Genoese artists, Niccolò and Sebastiano Roccatagliata. The main altar of the church is an elaborate Baroque creation by Tremignon decorated with sculptures by Meyring. In the choir are 16th century carved wooden choir stalls. The left chapel contains two especially noteworthy works, the *Last Supper* by Palma the Younger and the *Washing of the Feet*, a late work by Jacopo Tintoretto.

We cross the picturesque **Rio San Moise** and go down the **Calle Larga 22 Marzo 1848** and from here turn right into the **Calle delle Veste** which crosses the rio of the same name which leads to the **Campo San Fantin**. The lovely **church of San Fantin**, was designed by Scarpagnino in the 1500s. The interior with three naves marked by elegant Corinthian columns is a splendid Renaissance creation. Opposite the church is the renowned **La Fenice Theater.** Built at the end of the 18th century in an elegant neo-Classical style, the theater has always been one of the hubs of Venice's cultural and artistic life, but it was destroyed by the fire in 1996. Returning to Calle Larga 22 Marzo 1848, by way of the Calle delle Veste, we turn right and cross the **Rio dell'Albero** and proceed to the **Campo Santa Maria Zobenigo** and the church of the same name.

THE CHURCH OF SANTA MARIA ZOBENIGO

The church was named for the family that commissioned it in the 9th century. In the niches on either side of the portal of Giuseppe Sardi's elaborate Baroque facade (1678-1683) are statues of members of the Barbaro family, who financed the restoration of the building in the 17th century. The relief views of the cities of *Zara, Candia, Padua, Rome, Corfù*, and *Spalato* are of considerable interest.

● THE INTERIOR

The rectangular church has paintings on the ceiling by A. Zanchi. To the right is the interesting **Molin Chapel** whose ceiling painting of the *Virgin* has been attributed to Domenico Tintoretto. On the wall is the *Climb to Calvary* ascribed to Fontebasso. At the second altar is a *statue of the Blessed Gregorio Barbarigo* by Morlaiter, at the

third a *Visitation* by Palma the Younger. In the 18th century sacristy is a Rubens paintings, the *Virgin and Child with St. John*. In the choir, the *monument to Marco Giulio Contarini* by Vittoria, on the main altar, *statues of the Virgin Annunciate* and the *Angel Gabriel* by E. Meyring. In the third altar on the left, *Christ and St. Justine and St. Francis de Paul* by Jacopo Tintoretto.

We continue our itinerary crossing the **Rio Santa Maria Zobenigo**, the **Campiello della Feltrina**, and the **Rio di San Maurizio** to reach the **Campo di San Maurizio** and the **Calle dei Piovan**, the site of the **Scuola degli Albanesi**. The façade, built in 1531, is adorned with reliefs depicting the *Virgin and Child, St. Gallo* and *St. Maurice*: above is the *Sultan Mohammed Observing the Scutari Castle*. After crossing the **Rio di Santo Stefano** we take the **Calle del Spezier** which brings us to the **Campo Francesco Morosini** (or the Campo Santo Stefano). In the center of the huge square is a *monument to Niccolò Tommaseo*. Noteworthy among the buildings around the square are the 17th century **Palazzo Morosini**, the elegant Renaissance **Palazzo Loredan**, and two churches, Santo Stefano on the right and San Vitale on the left.

✝ THE CHURCH OF SANTO STEFANO

This late 13th century Romanesque-Gothic church has been restored many times over the centuries. The façade has distinctive single and double mullioned windows and a fine International Style portal executed by the Bon brothers.

● THE INTERIOR

The striking interior has aisles set off by columns of Greek marble and red marble from Verona and a beamed ceiling. A number of art treasures are to be found here. In the sacristy are three Tintorettos: the *Last Supper*, the *Washing of the Feet* and *Christ in the Garden of Gethsemane*. The *altarpiece* depicting *St. Peter and St. Lawrence* is by Bartolomeo Vivarini, the *Archangel Raphael and Saints* by Piazzetta and the *Virgin with Saints* by Palma the Elder. In the choir in the huge polygonal apse are magnificent 15th century Gothic *choir stalls*. From the left aisle we enter the splendid 16th century cloister, attributed to Scarpagnino, which was once adorned with frescoes by Pordenone.

On the other side of the Campo Morosini, is the **church of San Vitale** on the right. The original church was remodeled in the 17th century by Andrea Tirali in the style of Palladio. Inside are works by Piazzetta and St. Vitale on horseback with eight *saints* by Carpaccio. From the **Campo San Vidal** we cross the Grand Canal at the **Ponte dell'Accademia**. We are now in the **Campo della Carital** right in front of the Academy Galleries.

The Ponte della'Accademia.

The entrance to the Academy.

 ## THE ACADEMY GALLERIES

Five hundred years of Venetian art are on exhibit in the Accademia which, for homogenity, clarity of exposition, and quality, cannot be equalled anywhere. Its origins go back to 1750 when the Republic of St. Mark decided to

endow the city with an "Accademia di Pittori e scultori" (Academy of Painters and Sculptors) under the direction of Piazzetta. The original Academy occupied the Fondachetto delle Farine (Flour Storehouse), today the Port Authority, situated by the gardens of the former Royal Palace overlooking the harbor of St. Mark. In 1756 the Academy was granted official recognition and Piazzetta, by then an old man, decided to leave it in the capable hands of Giovan Battista Tiepolo. This was the core of the first group of works done by the pupils of the Academy. In 1807, during the French occupation, it was decided to transfer the art school and the works displayed in it to a more

fitting place and the choice fell upon the Scuola and Church of the Carità (in the Campo della Carità) and upon the former monastery of the Lateranense Canons, a building designed by Palladio in 1560 (but greatly altered since then). The collection thereafter considerably expanded as numerous works from suppressed churches and monasteries continuously poured in. During the period 1816-1856 bequests from Molin, Contarini, Venier, and Manfrin brought in new treasures. Lastly, several works returned from Austria after the Treaty of St. Germain was signed in 1919, and still other outstanding works were purchased by the Italian State under the directorship of Giulio Cantalamessa and Gino Fogolari. Somebody always asks why the name of the museum is Academy Galleries in the plural, even though there is only a single museum. Actually, the museum originally had two separate sections, one for paintings and the other for plaster casts used by the art students and the plural name has remained.

ROOM 1 - This splendid room is reached by a monumental staircase built in 1765 and adorned with two fine allegorical statues by Morlaiter. The stupendous gilded carved ceiling frames paintings by Alvise Vivarini and Campagnola. The room is devoted to 14th and 15th century Venetian school paintings. Of special note is the impressive *altarpiece* by Paolo Veneziano, still full of Byzantine influence. The subjects of the panels are the *Coronation of the Virgin* and *Scenes from the Lives of Christ and St. Francis*. Other fine works include the *Coronation of the Virgin* and *Justice between the Archangels Michael and Gabriel* by Jacobello del Fiore (1438) and the *Mystic Marriage of St. Catherine*, plus a superb altarpiece with the *Annunciation*, *Saints*, and *Prophets* by Lorenzo Veneziano. In the center of the hall is a splendid example of 15th century Venetian goldsmithing, the *Astylar Cross of St. Theodore*.

St. Jerome and a Believer, by *Piero della Francesca* (1450 c.); below: *the Virgin of the Zodiac,* by *Cosmè Tura* (1450 c.).

ROOM 2 - The late 15th-early 16th century Venetian school. Several of the masterpieces of Giovanni Bellini, renowned for his skillful use of color and feeling for the mystical, are in the Academy collection. These include the *Sacra Conversazione* (originally in the church of San Giobbe) and the *Lamentation*. The *Presentation at the Temple* and *Crucifixion of the 10.000 Martyrs on Mount Arafat* are by Carpaccio.

ROOM 3 - Cima da Conegliano and Giorgione. The *Female Nude* painted by Giorgione in 1508 is unfortunately in very poor condition.

ROOM 4 - The major works are a *Virgin and Child with Sts. Paul and George,* a *Virgin and Child with Sts. Catherine and Mary Magdalene,* and a *Virgin with Sleeping Babe* by Giovanni Bellini, the *Virgin of the Zodiac* by Cosme Tura, and *St. Jerome* by Piero della Francesca (c. 1450).

The Tempest, by *Giorgione* (1507 c.)
Preceding page: **Saint George,** by *A. Mantegna* (1468 c.).

The *St. George* by Mantegna, despite its tiny size, conveys a great sense of monumentality and physical strength.

ROOM 5 - This room contains Giorgione's splendid much-discussed painting of the *Tempest* full of symbolism and bathed in an atmosphere of liyric melancholy. In addition, there are several more superb Bellinis including the *Madonna degli Alberelli,* the *Pietà,* and the *Virgin and Child with St. John the Baptist* and a *Female Saint.*

The Pietà, by *G. Bellini*.

ROOM 6 - Paris Bordone painted the *Presentation of the Ring to the Doge,* which recounts a *miracle of St. Mark,* against a splendid background showing 16th century Venetian life. Other important works are the *Banquet of the Dives* by Bonifacio de' Pitati, *St. John the Baptist* by Titian, and the *Madonna dei Tesorieri* by Jacopo Tintoretto (1566).

The Banquet of Epulone, by *Bonifacio de'Pitati* (1540 c.).

ROOM 7 - Lorenzo Lotto's *Portrait of a Gentleman* reveals the painter's penetrating insight into the sitter's personality. Savoldo painted the *St. Anthony the Abbot with St. Paul, the Hermit.* The figures convey great solemnity and nobility.

ROOM 8 - Titian might have had a hand in this *Sacra Conversazione* regarded as Palma the Elder's masterpiece (1525). Also of note are Bonifacio de' Pitati's *Slaughter of the Innocents* and Romanino's *Pietà.*

ROOM 9 - Titian's school. The most interesting works are *God the Father Blessing Venice* and the *Virgin and Child with Saints* by Bonifacio de' Pitati. The *Evangelists' Symbols* are from Titian's workshop.

Portrait of a Gentleman, by *L. Lotto* (1526 c.).

Pietà, by *Titian.*

ROOM 10 - The 16th century Venetian school. This room contains several of the museum's major works from the height of the Venetian Renaissance. On of the most striking is the *Banquet in the House of Levi* which Paolo Veronese painted in 1573. The painter had intended this elaborate picture to represent the Last Supper, but the Inquisition Court, decreeing that the setting and poses of some of the figures were unbefitting to such a serious subject, compelled him to change the title. The *Miracle of the Slave,* painted by Tintoretto in 1548, was originally part of a whole cycle on the miracle of St. Mark. This work is a splendid example of Tintoretto's skill in using dynamic compositional patterns, emphasized by dramatic treatment of light and shade, which made him one of the greatest of the 16th century Venetian masters. The *Pietà* by Titian, commissioned for the church of the Frari, was the last work the master painted before his death in 1576. The dissolving forms and broader brushstroke are typical of Titian's late style.

ROOM 11 - The room is divided into two sections. In the first are *Adam and Eve,* the *Creation of the Animals,* and *Cain and Abel* by Tintoretto, and the *Mystic Marriage of St. Catherine* by Veronese. In the second are 16th and 17th century works by painters such as Tiepolo, Luca Giordano, and Pietro da Cortona.

ROOM 12 - The 17th century Venetian school. The highlights include several *Landscapes* by Marco Ricci, the *Rape of Europa* by Zuccarelli, and *Landscapes* by Giuseppe Zais.

ROOM 13 - The most interesting paintings are the *Rest on the Flight to Egypt* and the *Virgin in Glory with St. Jerome* by Jacopo Bassano, the *Virgin and Child and Four Senators* and three *portraits of Procuratori* (magistrates) by Tintoretto, and *Deucalion and Pyrrha, Christ and Pilate,* and the *Presentation in the Temple* by Schiavone.

St. Jerome, by *Jacopo Bassano* (detail).

The Rape of Europa, by *F. Zuccarelli* (1745 c.)

ROOM 14 - Noteworthy are several canvases by the Roman painter, Domenico Feti, including *David, Girl Reading, Meditation,* and *Isaac and Jacob.* Jan Liss painted the *Sleeping Turk,* the *Sacrifice of Isaac,* and *Apollo and Marsyas.*

ROOM 15 - 18th century works by Tiepolo, Solimena, and others.

ROOM 16 - In addition to superb Tiepolos, this room also contains the *Fortuneteller* by Piazzetta, one of the best-known Venetian genre painters of the 18th century.

The Fortune Teller, by *G.B. Piazzetta* (1740).

Portico and Courtyard, by *Canaletto* (1763).

ROOM 17 - Antonio Canale, better known as Canaletto, is the foremost painter of the Venetian school called "*vedutismo*" (views). His pictures, painted in a crystal clear, terse style, appear as mirror-like reflections of reality. Paintings of his favorite subject, views of Venice, can be throughout European museums. In this room is a *View of Venice* dating from 1765. The other renowned "*vedutista*" is Francesco Guardi, although his style stressing broad brushstroke and a warm palette differs greatly from Canaletto's. Guardi is represented here by the *View of the Island of San Giorgio*. The delightful genre scenes of everyday life in 18th century Venice are by Pietro Longhi (the *Dancing lesson*, the *Concert*, the *Toilette*) and Rosalba Carriera (*Selfportrait*, the *French Lady*, and *Portrait of a Youth*). The room also contains a series of attractive drawings by Sebastiano Ricci, Piazzetta, and Giambattista Pittoni.

Aesculapius' Dream, by *S. Ricci* (1710 ca.); below: **View of the Island of San Giorgio**, by *F. Guardi*.

Portrait of a Young Man, by *Rosalba Carriera.*

ROOM 18 - 18th century paintings and sculpture. Of special interest are two sculptures, *Apollo and Wrestlers,* which are Antonio Canova's trial pieces when, at the age of eighteen, he applied for admission to the Accademia Art School, and a *St. Joseph with Child and Saints* by Tiepolo.

ROOM 19 - We return to the 15th century. The splendid *Flagellated Christ* is by Antonello da Saliba.

ROOM 20 - Mostly paintings by Gentile Bellini, Giovanni's brother. Influenced by Mantegna, Gentile loved huge compositions illustrating the magnificence of Venetian public life in the 15th century: the *Processions in Piazza San Marco* (1496) we see here is a fascinating historical document as well as an outstanding work of art. The *Miraculous Healing of a Possessed man* by Vittore Carpaccio reveals the master's extraordinary narrative skill.

ROOM 21 - These wall-size paintings are part of a cycle on the theme of the *Legend of St. Ursula* painted by Carpaccio at the end of 1400s (1490-1496) for the Scuola di Sant'Orsola which was suppressed at the time of the French occupation in the late 1790s. The story of Ursula, the virgin princess from Brittany martyred during the Huns' siege of Cologne, is narrated in Carpaccio's inimitable style, combining fanciful flights of imagination with careful observation of down-to-earth everyday detail.

ROOM 22 - We cross this early 19th century neo-Classical room on our way back to Room 18 from which we enter the huge hall which was once the upper part of the former church of Santa Maria della Carità.

ROOM 23 - This room features more 15th century paintings. The highlights include Giovanni Bellini's four *triptychs*. Carlo Crivelli's four *saints,* and an *altarpiece* by Bartolomeo Vivarini depicting the *Nativity, Pietà* and *Angels* and *Saints.*

ROOM 24 - Originally the pilgrims' lodgings of the Scuola della Carità, this room has an impressive gilded carved ceiling. The outstanding work on display is undoubtedly Titian's *Presentation in the Temple*. This work was painted in 1538 when Titian had reached full artistic maturity.

The English Ambassadors at the Court of Brittany, by *V. Carpaccio* (1495 ca.).

NINTH ITINERARY

• •

Palazzo Rezzonico, *headquarters of the Museo del Settecento Veneziano.*

THE MUSEUM OF 18TH CENTURY VENICE

The museum is inside the Palazzo Rezzonico overlooking the Grand Canal. The palace, originally belonging to a noble Venetian family, Rezzonico was the last home of Robert Browning. The City of Venice purchased it in 1935 and used it for the reconstruction of the interior of an 18th Century patrician dwelling.

A visit to the museum is the best way to get an idea of what Venice was actually like in the fascinating 1700s, the period so wittily recounted in Carlo Goldoni's plays and on Pietro Longhi's charming canvases.

Lacquered "chinoiserie" chest; below: *console with gilded cupids.*

From the atrium we take the monumental staircase up to the second floor. The first room we see is the huge Ballroom adorned with magnificent furniture carved by Brustolon. We then enter the **Sala dell'Allegoria Nuziale** (Room of the Nuptial Allegory) which was named after Tiepolo's painting of the *Marriage of Ludovico Rezzonico.* The **Sala dei Pastelli** (Pastel Room) contains several of Rosalba Carriera's delicate works. In the **Sala degli Arazzi** (Tapestry Room) are splendid Flemish tapestries. The **Sala del Trono** (Throne Room), originally the nuptial chamber, has a fresco in the middle by Tiepolo and, due to the splendor and magnificence of its furnishings, is one of the most elaborate in the palace. The **Sala del Tiepolo** (Tiepolo Room) is adorned with an allegorical fresco by the master representing *Fortune and Wisdom.* The library has ceiling paintings by Francesco Maffei. The **Sala dei Lazzarini** received its name from the two impressive paintings by the Lazzarini adorning it. The **Sala del Brustolon** features the Venetian master-craftsman's exquisite carved furniture and a sculpture collection. Third floor: The **Portego dei Dipinti** (Picture Hall) contains a collection of 18th century Venetian school paintings, including Piazzetta's *Self-portrait* and *Death of Darius.* Jan Liss' *Judith and Holofernes,* and several *Landscapes* by Giuseppe Zais. The **Sala del Longhi** (Longhi Room) contains 34 fascinating genre scenes of 18th century Venetian life by Pietro Longhi. The ceiling painting of *Zephyr and Flora* is by Tiepolo. After passing through two rooms frescoed by Guardi, we enter a delightful reconstruction of an 18th century Venetian bedroom. Two little rooms lead to another reconstruction, this one a re-creation of the Villa dei Tiepolo (Tiepolo Mansion) in Zianigo. These frescoes, all of which originally adorned the villa, are by Domenico Tiepolo, son of Giovan Battista. Also of interest are the **Camera dei Pagliacci** (Clown Room), the **chapel** (frescoed by the young Tiepolo in 1749), and the not-to-be-missed **Sala del Ridotto** which contains two renowned paintings by Guardi, the *Convent Parlor,* and the *Sala del Ridotto*. On the fourth floor is a reconstruction of an old Venetian pharmacy and a marionette theater.

Taking the **Fondamenta Rezzonico** behind the palace, we soon reach the **Campo di San Barnaba**.

The Spinner, by *Longhi.*

THE CHURCH OF SAN BARNABA

The church was erected between 1749 and 1776 by Lorenzo Boschetti. The simple façade, inspired by Classical models, consists of tall columns surmounted by a tympanum. The handsome 14th century brick belltower has a cone-shaped cusp.

● THE INTERIOR

The interior is adorned with Corinthian columns set into the nave walls. The ceiling was frescoed by a follower of Tiepolo's, Costantino Cedini, and shows *St. Barnabas in Glory*. The *Birth of the Virgin* by Foler is at the first altar on the right although the most interesting works are in the choir: *St. Barnabas and Other Saints* by Damiano Mazzo on the main altar, the *Ascent to Calvary* and the *Last Supper* by Palma the Younger on the walls, and, above the altar, a painting of the *Holy Family* by Paolo Veronese.

We cross back over the picturesque **Rio di San Barnaba,** with its busy boat traffic turn left into the **Fondamenta Alberti,** and then right into the **Rio Terrà Canal.** On the left side we soon come to the **Campo Santa Margherita** and the church of the Carmini.

The church of San Barnaba.

The picturesque Rio di San Barnaba.

THE CHURCH OF THE CARMINI

S ebastiano Mariani added a Renaissance facade to this 14th century church at the beginning of the 15th century. A portal proceeded by a porch has been preserved from the original building on the left side. The belltower dates from the 17th century.

● THE INTERIOR

The aisles are set off from the nave by fine 14th century columns with beautifully carved capitals. The extensive fresco cycle of episodes from the *History of the Carmelite Order* was executed by various artists between the second half of the 17th and first half of the 18th centuries. Among the art treasures contained in the church are the *altarpiece* with the *Adoration of the Shepherds, Sts. Helen, Catherine,* and *Tobias and the Angel* by Cima da Conegliano (second bay of the right aisle), a relief with the *Deposition* by Francesco di Giorgio Martini (in the sacristy) and *St. Nicholas and Other Saints* by Lorenzo Lotto (second bay on the left aisle).

173

THE SCUOLA GRANDE OF THE CARMINI

This attractive building on the right side of the Carmini church has been attributed to Baldassarre Longhena (1688). By the altar on the ground floor hall is the *Assumption of the Virgin* by S. Piatti. The large paintings on the walls are by N. Bambini and represent: the *Flight into Egypt*, the *Birth of the Virgin* and the *Circumcision of Christ.* In the main hall of the upper floor, in addition to works by less important artists, is a magnificent ceiling composed of nine canvases painted by Tiepolo between 1739 and 1744 when he was at the height of his artistic maturity. The center panel portrays: *Our Lady of Carmel Handing Blessed Simone Stok the Scapular Surrounded by Virtues and Angels in Flight.* It conveys an incredible effect of grace and luminosity. The **Sala dell'Albergo** contains *New Testament Scenes* on the walls by A. Balestra and a painting of the *Assumption of the Virgin* by Padovanino on the ceiling. In the corridor leading to the **Sala dell'Archivio**, adorned with works by lesser known artists, is *Judith and Holofernes,* the masterpiece by Piazzetta.

THE CHURCH OF SAN SEBASTIANO

The church was built in the 1500s by an architect from Cremona, Francesco da Castiglione, who was helped by Scarpagnino. It was restored in 1867. Inside is the finest collection of Veronese's paintings to be found anywhere in Venice. (Veronese himself was buried in the church in 1588).

 THE INTERIOR

The decoration of this church was commissioned from Paolo Veronese whose exuberant youth and vigor are plainly visible. Unfortunately Veronese was confined to a wall space that hardly lent itself to fresco painting so he had to overcome difficult technical problems relating to poor lighting and tight spaces. The most noteworthy paintings are the *Story of Esther* in the ceiling panels, the *Virgin with St. Sebastian and Other Saints* by the altar of the main chapel, the *Martyrdom of Sts. Mark and Marcellinus* on the left the *Martyrdom of St. Sebastian* on the right, and the *Annunciation* on the triumphal arch. In the chapel to the left of the main chapel are a *bust of Veronese* and, on the ground, his *tomb slab*, as well as an *organ* with panels decorated by the great master. The sacristy contains paintings by various followers of Veronese and, on the ceiling, five panels which were the first works the great artist from Verona did in Venice. After the third altar on the right is a grandiose *monument to Bishop Livio Podocataro* executed by Sansovino in 1556.

We go back over the **Rio San Sebastiano** and turn right, continuing along the canal on the **Fondamenta San Basilio**, passing **Campo San Basegio** until we reach the **Zattere al Ponte Lungo.** Here we turn right, proceeding along the **Rio San Trovaso** and, after crossing the **Rio d'Ognissanti**, we reach the **Campo San Trovaso** and the church of the same name.

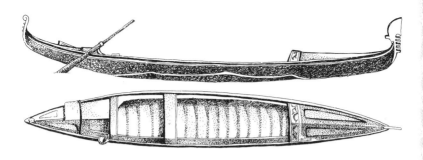

THE CHURCH OF SAN TROVASO

This is Venetian dialect for Gervasio and Protasio, names of two important saints. Already in existence by the 11th century, the church was burnt to the ground and rebuilt in the Palladian neo-Classical style in 1583.

● THE INTERIOR

The interior has a huge choir and side chapels. At the third altar on the right is *St. Francis de Paul, Faith and Charity,* by Alvise di Friso. On the wall nearby is a *Virgin and Child* by a follower of Giovanni Bellini. In the right transept is a lovely altar frontal, a Renaissance relief attributed to Pietro Lombardo which portrays *Angels with the Symbols of the Passion.* In the chapel to the right of the main chapel is a *Crucifixion* by Domenico Tintoretto on

The church of San Trovaso; below: a charming rio at San Trovaso.

the altar. A Gothic masterpiece, *St. Chrysogonus on Horseback* adorns the walls. It has been attributed by some to Jacobello del Fiore and by others to Michele Giambono. The choir contains the *Adoration of the Magi* and *Joachim Expelled from the Temple* by Jacopo Tintoretto and his pupils. In the chapel to the left of the main chapel is a *Temptation of St. Anthony* by Jacopo Tintoretto. The sacristy contains a *Virgin* by Rosalba Carriera and *Sts. John and Mary Magdalene* attributed to Tintoretto. In the Chapel of the Blessed Sacrament in the left transept are paintings by Tintoretto (the *Last Supper* and the *Washing of the Feet*) and Palma the Younger (the *Deposition* on the nearby altar).

The "squero" of San Trovaso,
the picturesque district where gondolas are built and repaired.

Going back to the zattere, we cross **Ponte Lungo** and walk along the **Zattere ai Gesuati.** On the left we pass by the **church of Santa Maria della Visitazione**, noting its lovely 16th century façade, and soon after arrive at the church of the Gesuati.

THE CHURCH OF I GESUATI

Known also as Santa Maria del Rosario, the church was erected between 1726 and 1743 for the Dominican friars who commissioned the architect Giorgio Massari to design it for the site of what once was a 14th century monastery called the "Monastery of the Poor Gesuati". The façade is a handsome interpretation of the Classical style.

● THE INTERIOR

The elliptical-shaped church has a domed choir and side chapels. The ceiling frescoes by G. B. Tiepolo represent *St. Dominic in Glory,* the *Institution of the Rosary, St. Dominic and the Virgin,* and the *Mysteries of the Rosary.* Starting our tour of the altars from the right side, first altar, the *Virgin in Glory with Three Saints,* a masterpiece painted by Tiepolo in 1747, and second altar, *St. Dominic,* by G. B. Piazzetta (1739). The dome frescoes in the choir are by Tiepolo. The main altar and choir stalls are fine 18th century works. The *Virgin and St. Anne* was painted by M. Ignoli. On the left side (third altar) is a *Crucifixion* by Tintoretto.

TENTH ITINERARY

●●●●●●●●●●●●●●●●●●●●●●●●

This itinerary starts out at the church of Santa Maria della Salute which majestically dominates the last stretch of the Grand Canal.

The church of Santa Maria della Salute.

THE CHURCH OF SANTA MARIA DELLA SALUTE

The vicissitudes throughout the construction of the church were many and varied: here we shall try to recount the most interesting ones. In 1630 Venice was struck by a terrible plague which caused thousands to perish. The Senate thus decided that, should Divine Providence intercede on the city's behalf, the citizenry would erect a huge church in honor of the Virgin. The plague ended and the Senate announced a competition for the design of the church. All of the outstanding architects of the day took part and the project was awarded to a young man, Baldassarre Longhena. Work began in 1631, but soon grave difficulties set in. First of all, the terrain was unable to support the weight of the building going up and began to give way. Longhena solved the problem by inserting a host of supporting beams deep into the soil. But his troubles were not yet over. When the central dome was about to be set up, it looked as though the walls, would be unabie to bear its weight. Longhena thought up an ingenious solution: he added a series of curlicue braces to help support the drum upon which the dome rests and which give the church its unique and distinctive appearance. By the time the church could be consecrated in 1687, Baldassare Longhena was five years dead. Ever since, on November 21 each year, a picturesque procession, in which the whole city of Venice takes part, is held. On this occasion, a bridge connecting the church to the opposite shore is put up. The church has an octagonal plan and is surmounted by a great dome and a smaller dome directly over the choir.

177

Aerial view of the Punta della Dogana,
and the church of Santa Maria della Salute.

● THE INTERIOR

Simple yet grandiose, the interior is shaped like an octagon over which rises the great dome. It has six side chapels. At the first right-hand altars are paintings by Luca Giordano recounting the *Story of Mary*: the *Presentation of Virgin at the Temple*, the *Assumption* and the *Nativity of the Virgin*. At the third altar on the left is a late work by Titian, the *Pentecost*. The marble sculpture on the main altar represents the *Plague Fleeing Before the Virgin* and is by Giusto Le Court. The large sacristy contains a wealth of unforgettable Titian masterpieces: the *Death of Abel*, the *Sacrifice of Abraham*, and *David and Goliath*, dated 1543 on the ceiling, and over the altar, a youthful work of 1512, *St. Mark and Other Saints*. The works of other artists adorn the walls. Outstanding among these is one of Tintoretto's most famous paintings, the *Wedding at Cana*.

Above: *the interior of the church of Santa Maria della Salute*; right: *the inside of the dome.*

Next page: *the façade of the church of Santa Maria della Salute.*

Palazzo Venier dei Leoni, home of the Guggenheim Collection of Modern Art.

Crossing the **Ponte della Salute** to our left when we leave the church, we take the calle leading into the tiny, charming **Campo San Gregorio.** Continuing along the **Calle San Giorgio** and then the **Calle del Bastion**, we cross the **Rio della Fornace**. Then, proceeding along the **Calle Barbaro** and the **Calle San Cristoforo**, filled with glassblowers' shops, we come to the **Palazzo Venier dei Leoni** whose façade overlooks the Grand Canal. This is the Peggy Guggenheim Collection of Modern Art.

🏛 THE PEGGY GUGGENHEIM COLLECTION

The Peggy Guggenheim Collection is a museum of modern art, established by the American heiress Peggy Guggenheim (1898-1979). She acquired the most important part of the collection (for the purpose of creating a museum of contemporary art) between 1938 and 1947 in London, Paris and New York. In 1942 she opened the gallery-museum Art of This Century in New York, where she exhibited her own collection of European avant-garde works and organized several shows dedicated to young American artists, such as Motherwell, Rotko, Still and Pollock. The collection was shown in Europe for the first time at the Biennale di Venezia in 1948. The following year, Peggy bought the Palazzo Venier dei Leoni, an unfinished XVIII century building on the Grand Canal, where she lived for 30 years, and opened her home to visitors as a museum.

The collection, built up following the advice of artists and critics such as Marcel Duchamp and Herbert Read, and her second husband the German surrealist, Max Ernst, is one of the greatest collections of its kind in the world. In 1976, a few years before she died, Peggy bequeathed the palazzo and the collection to the Solomon R. Guggenheim Foundation, which now manages it along with the Guggenheim museums in New York and Bilbao in Spain.

The Nasher Sculpture Garden contains works by Giacometti (*Woman Standing*), Raymond Duchamp-Villon (*The Horse*) and Henry Moore, Jean Arp and Max Ernst. Two inscriptions behind the gazebo, tell where the ashes of Peggy Guggenheim and her little dogs are buried. In the building, the entrance room contains many important works by Picasso (*On the Beach* and *The Studio*) and a *Mobile* by Alexander Calder. From the entrance we can go to the terrace overlooking the Grand Canal and admire Marino Marini's *The Angel of the City*. Going back inside, the collection continues with important pieces by masters of cubism, Picasso (*The Poet*), Braque (*The Clarinet Player*), Léger, Duchamp, Gris, Gleizes, Metzinger and Delaunay. Early Italian Modernism is represented by the Futurists, (Boccioni, Balla and Severini) and the metaphysical painter Giorgio De Chirico (*The Red Tower*). The Europen Abstract movement is represented by Kupka, Kandinsky (*Landscape with Red Spots* and the *White Cross*), Mondrian, Van Doesburg, Malevich, Pevsner, Lissitzky and Hélion. The are works by Arp, Picabia, Schwitters, and Ernst from

Dynamism of a Galloping Horse with Houses, by *Umberto Boccioni* (1914-15).

Untitled, by *Kazimir Malevich* (ca.1916).

the Dada movement, while the fantastic elements in the works by Chagall (*The Rain*) and Klee (*Magic Garden*) link these artists Surrealism which is well represented by Ernst (*The Kiss, Dressing the Bride, The Antipope*), Miró (*Dutch Interior II, Seated Woman II*), Magritte (*Empire of Light*), Delvaux, Dalì (*The Birth of Liquid Desires*), Tanguy, Comell, Brauner, Matta and others. The support that Peggy Guggenheim gave young American artists in the 'forties, is documented by paintings by Jackson Pollock (*The Moon Woman, Alchemistry*), young works by Motherwell, Rothko, Baziotes and Still and a large painting by Gorky. Post-war European Art is represented by Bacon, Dubuffet, Vedova, Fontana, Jorn, Appel, Nicholson, Sutherland, Bacci, Tancredi and many others. The collection also includes important sculptures: two bronzes by Brancusi (*Maiastra, Bird in Space*), works by Giacometti (*Woman Walking, Woman with Slit Throat*). The headboard from Peggy Guggenheim's bed is a unique piece by Alexander Calder.

The museum hosts many modern shows; there is also a **Museum Shop** and a **Museum Cafè** in the new wing, as well as the large, shaded garden which is open according to the museum's schedule.

Leaving the Guggenheim collection, we take the **Fondamenta Venier,** making a right and following the **Rio delle Torresella.** We then proceed along the **Calle della Chiesa** until we reach the **Campo San Vio** where we turn left into the **Fondamenta Bragadin,** continuing along the **Rio di San Vio** until we reach the **Zattere ai Gesuati.** Here we turn right and walk to the vaporetto station where we take a boat crossing the Giudecca canal to reach the charming **Isle of the Giudecca,** a populous suburb of Venice, whose name probably derives from the fact that it was once the neighborhood set aside for the Jews (giudei). It is composed of eight little islands joined by bridges. A brief excursion to the Giudecca, immersed in silence and greenery, is a relaxing pause from our strenuous sightseeing.

The typical Rio di San Vio; below: *the Canale della Giudecca.*

The ferry goes from the Gesuati, docking at the **Fondamenta Sant'Eufemia,** on the Giudecca not far from the **church of Sant'Eufemia.** Although the original core dates from the 9th century, the building has been extensively remodeled over the centuries. On the 16th century portico beside the church is an interesting Byzantine style lunette on which a *Crucifixion* is depicted. Inside the church are fine Venetian-Byzantine capitals dating from the 11th century. Continuing along the **Fondamenta Ponte Piccolo** and the **Fondamenta San Giacomo** we soon reach the church of the Redentore.

The Rio delle Torresella.

THE CHURCH OF IL REDENTORE

T he church is the result of Andrea Palladio's architectural genius combined with the technical skill of Antonio Da Ponte who built it between 1577 and 1592. It was put up in thanksgiving for the cessation of another of the innumerable plague epidemics which had taken its toll of Venetian victims. A huge staircase leads up to a façade proper which consists of a single order of columns surmounted by a tympanum. Crowning the church is a dome flanked by a pair of belltowers.

The church of the Redentore.

● THE INTERIOR

T he inside reflects the classical harmony of the outside. The stately colonnade along the interior confers a majestic effect to the whole. The Baroque main altar is adorned with bronzes by Campagna. In the sacristy are some interesting works, including a *Virgin and Child* by Alvise Vivarini, a *Baptism of Christ* by a follower of Veronese, a *Virgin and Child with Saints* by Palma the Younger, and several works by Bassano.

185

Aerial view of the island of San Giorgio Maggiore.

Proceeding along the **Fondamenta della Croce** and the **Fondamenta delle Zitelle**, we arrive, opposite the church of the same name, at the vaporetto station for the **Isle of San Giorgio Maggiore** which is a landmark in the middle of the harbor of San Marco. On the island are the church and monastery of San Giorgio Maggiore.

THE CHURCH OF SAN GIORGIO MAGGIORE

The church's stark white façade stands out impressively against the ochre-hued buildings crowding it. One of Palladio's finest designs (the great architect worked on the project between 1565 and 1580), the basilica was finished in 1610 by Scamozzi who, however, followed the master's original plans. The façade once more reveals Palladio's distinctive style: the space is divided into three sections by four columns topped by Corinthian capitals. In the two niches between the columns are *statues of Sts. George and Stephen* and, on either side *busts of Doges Tribuno Mommo and P. Zini* by Giulio Moro. The belltower was put up by the Bolognese architect Benedetto Buratti in 1791 to replace an older one which collapsed in 1773. From its top there is an unforgettable view of the city and the lagoon below.

186

● THE INTERIOR

Unadorned yet imposing, the church is in the shape of an inverted Latin cross. In the second altar on the right is a wooden *Crucifix* by the great Florentine artist, Michelozzo. On the main altar of the choir is a superb bronze group by Girolamo Campagna (1593). Two great Tintorettos are hanging on the walls: the *Last Supper* on the right and the *Shower of Manna* on the left. In the apse are magnificent carved wooden choir stalls dated 1598.

The **Benedictine monastery,** of extremely ancient origin, has had famous guests such as Frederick II of Sweden and Cosimo de' Medici. Recently thoroughly restored, the building is now the headquarters of the **Fondazione Giorgio Cini,** an internationally renowned artistic and cultural foundation. One of the highlights of our tour of the monastery is the **Chiostro del Palladio**. The cloister is a superb example of Palladio's simple, elegant style. In the **Cenacolo** (refectory) there is also a fine painting by Tintoretto, the *Marriage of the Virgin*.

Above: *the façade of the church of San Giorgio Maggior*e; below: *view of the Island of San Giorgio.* Next page: *a stunning twilight over the Punta della Dogana, seen from the Island of San Giorgio.*

ENVIRONS OF VENICE

The Lido.

*W*e shall now turn to the group of splendid islands which are like gemstones laid out amidst the lagoon, the most precious of which is Venice herself. There are all kinds, ranging in size from tiny uninhabited islets to good-sized islands, now sleepy fishing villages, but once thriving cities. An excursion to Torcello, Burano, and Murano is a must for those who would like to really know Venice. These island towns are fascinating not only for the art treasures they possess, but also for their hauntingly beautiful landscapes in an atmosphere of magical silence and this is not all the lagoon has to offer. We must not forget the local handicrafts; glassblowing, lacemaking, and coppercrafting are some of the typical ones practiced by the local artisans.

THE LIDO OF VENICE

The Lido is actually an elongated island about a mile from Venice, bordered by a considerable stretch of sandy beach. Once the city's natural defense, it is now a celebrated resort. The Lido's international reputation comes from its superbly equipped hotels and excellent tourist accommodations, its fine beach, and the cultural, artistic, and sports events held here throughout the year, with the greatest concentration, of course, in summer.

From the smart sophistication of the Lido with its elegant hotels and bathing establishments, we pass to the enchanting peace of the mysterious **Isle of San Lazzaro degli Armeni.** Here a community of Armenian monks has been thriving for centuries, immersed in the silence of their convent, surrounded by luxuriant vegetation. The atmosphere of the island is permeated with memories of Byron who spent lengthy periods of his life on San Lazzaro. Sailing towards Murano we encounter the **Island of San Michele in Isola** where, according to legend, St. Romualdo, founder of the Camaldolese Order once lived (although the order held on to the island until the 19th century, today it is just a sleepy cemetery marked by majestic cypresses). Proceeding toward Burano and Torcello we encounter, on the left, the solitary **Islet of San Giacomo in Palude** and, on the right, the lovely **Islet of San Francesco del Deserto**, where solitude and silence reign over the thick vegetation surrounding the hermitage. We shall now take a closer look at the major lagoon centers, Murano with its glass factories, Burano with its lace-making, and the former rival of Venice, Torcello.

MURANO

Less than a mile away from Venice, Murano is a typical lagoon town spread over five islets. It is renowned for its glassblowing industry which dates back to the

Bird's eye view of Murano.

13th century. The **Glass Museum** in the **Palazzo Giustiniani** exhibits rare pieces of the glassblower's art, including Roman and Egyptian objects, dating from Antiquity to the 18th century.

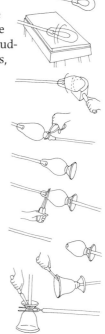

A typical rio on the Island of Murano.

THE CHURCH OF SAN PIETRO MARTIRE

Inside this 14th century church are numerous works of art. Three of the finest are Giovanni Bellini's *Virgin Enthroned with Two Angels and Saints* and *Assumption of the Virgin and Saints*, and Veronese's *St. Jerome in the Desert* over the sacristy door.

THE CHURCH OF SANTI MARIA E DONATO

The church originally on the site was rebuilt in the 12th century. It is a unique example of the Venetian-Byzantine style with its unusual hexagonal apse and double tier of columns creating a graceful pattern of niches and loggias.

Church of Santi Maria e Donato; below: the church façade.

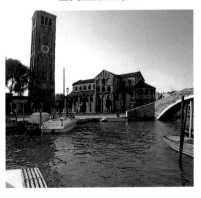

● THE INTERIOR

The church has a basilican plan and aisles set off from the nave by ten marble columns with superb Corinthian capitals. The marble flooring dates from the 12th century. At the beginning of the left-wall is a large painted carved *altarpiece* which is an outstanding example of 14th century Venetian art. The mosaic showing the *Virgin in Prayer Against a Gold Ground* in the semi-dome of the apse dates from the 12th century.

Aerial view of the Island of the Burano.

BURANO

Burano (originally Burianum or Boreanum) occupies four tiny islands inhabited mainly by fishermen. It was first settled in the 5th-6th centuries by refugees from Altinum fleeing Attila's fearful Huns. Though it is mostly famous for the traditional art of lacemaking which the women of the town have been handing down to their daughters for centuries, Burano also boasts noteworthy artistic treasures.

A typical rio on the Island of Burano.

On this page: *charming views of the Island of Burano.*

Taking the main road of the village named after its best-known native son, the 18th century composer Baldassarre Galuppi, known as *"Il Suranello,"* we soon reach the main square and the 16th century **church of San Martino**. Alongside is its eighteenth century belltower which, like the Tower of Pisa, leans dangerously to one side, and the **chapel of Santa Barbara** which contains works of great interest, such as Tiepolo's huge *Crucifixion* (dated c. 1725), *St. Mark and Other Saints* by Girolamo da Santacroce, and several canvases by Giovanni Mansueti (end of the 16th century). On the same square stands the **Palazzo della Podestà**, a 19th century building now occupied by the **Lacemaking School**, which was founded in 1872 so that this traditional art would never be lost.

Aerial view of the Island of Torcello.

TORCELLO

O nly six miles from Venice is one of the most fascinating spots in the lagoon. Now just a solitary village on a lonely island, it was once a flourishing hub of culture and commerce whose greatness dimmed as Venice's grew. All that is left of its long ago splendor is a group of monuments facing out on a picturesque grassy square around the so-called "*caregon*", which, if popular tradition is to be believed, was originally Attila's throne.

A picturesque rio on Torcello; right:*"Attila's Throne"*.

Above: *the Cathedral of Santa Maria Assunta*; right: *the bell tower.*

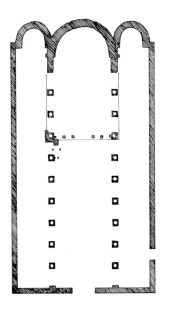

✞ THE CATHEDRAL

Dedicated to St. Maria Assunta, the Cathedral's origins go back to the year 639, although it was rebuilt in the early 11th century together with its majestic belltower. Ruins of a circular-plan 8th century baptistry are visible in front of the building.

● THE INTERIOR

Austere and simple, the church has aisles set off from the nave by columns. The inner façade is entirely covered with remarkable 12th-13th century Byzantine mosaics portraying the *Last Judgment.* In the nave are two pulpits and an iconostasis (rood screen) with exquisite transennae supporting a series of 15th century icons. In the triumphal arch is a 12th century mosaic representing the 12 *Apostles* and, in the semi-dome, one of the *Virgin and Child* dating from the 13th century.

The church of Santa Fosca and the adjacent cathedral of Santa Maria Assunta.

The church of Santa Fosca; right, top:
fragment of a coloumn; bottom: ***detail
of the portico that encircles the church.***

⛪ THE CHURCH OF SANTA FOSCA

The church, built around the 11th century, has an unusual octagonal shape. On the outside a portico resting on arches runs around five sides of the building, while the simple Greek cross interior has columns decorated with Byzantine capitals

The portico of the Palazzo dell'Archivo;
right: **The Virgin Praying,** *mosaic in the cathedral of Santa Maria Assunta* (XII cent.); below: **the Lion of St. Mark,** *fragment from the Palazzo del Consiglio.*

Fragments of the Palazzo del Consiglio from Altino.

On the square, are two Gothic buildings, the **Palazzo del Consiglio** and the **Palazzo dell'Archivio**. They contain a fascinating collection of archeological finds discovered on the lagoon islands, mainly Torcello.

USEFUL INFORMATION

This last part of the guidebook contains a compendium of useful information about the museums, hotels, restaurants, public and private services and whatever else may be of help in touring Venice.

- How to reach Venice: main trains - domestic and international flights
- Main sea connections in Venice
- Gondola stations
- Water taxis
- Baggage handlers
- Useful information
- Museums/Galleries/Exhibitions
- Banks
- Consulates
- Places of worship
- Cultural foundations and associations
- Pubs and piano bars
- Theaters and cinemas
- Venice by night
- Clubs
- Emergency phone numbers
- Hotels and restaurants in and around Venice
- Hostels in Venice
- Agritourism establishments
- Campsites
- Map of main sea routes and connections

MAIN TRAINS LEAVING VENICE

		ic	ic	ic	ic	ec	ic	ic	ic	ic	f		ic	f	WLc	WLcc				
VENICE	p.	6.05	6.18	8.05	10.05	11.05	12.05	13.05	14.05	14.18	16.05	16.58	17.18	18.05	18.31	19.18	20.05	20.18	21.18	22.02	23.28
MESTRE	p.	6.17	6.30	8.17	10.17	11.17	12.17	13.17	14.17	14.30	16.17	17.10	17.30	18.17	18.42	19.27	20.17	20.30	21.30	22.42	23.43
VERONA	a.	7.28	7.55	9.28	11.31	12.28	13.28	14.28	15.28	15.55	17.28	18.28	18.55	19.28	20.19	20.55	21.28	21.55	22.55	0.02	1.10
MILAN	a.	8.55	9.45	10.55	12.55	13.55	14.55	15.55	16.55	17.45	18.55	19.55	20.40	20.55	22.12	22.45	22.55	23.45	0.45	1.34	2.55
TURIN	a.	10.45	—	—	14.45	—	—	—	20.45	—	—										
GENOA	a.	—	12.40	—	—	—	18.42	—	—	—	22.40	—	—	—	—	5.15	—	5.15			

		P•	ic	ic	ic	ic	ec	ic	WLdn	ic	WLccd	WLccd	WLcc								
VENICE	p.	5.50	6.25	7.45	8.25	—	10.25	11.45	12.25	—	14.25	15.45	16.25	17.45	18.25	19.02	19.45	20.25	22.50		
MESTRE	p.	6.02	6.37	7.57	8.37	9.57	10.37	11.57	12.37	13.57	14.37	15.57	16.37	17.57	18.37	19.15	19.57	20.37	23.30	0.38	3.58
BOLOGNA	a.	7.38	8.23	9.35	10.50	11.35	12.23	13.35	14.23	15.35	16.23	17.35	18.23	19.35	20.23	21.10	21.35	22.23	1.40	2.40	5.40
FLORENCE	a.	8.37	—	10.42	—	12.42	—	14.42	—	16.42	—	18.42	—	20.42	—	22.41	22.47	—	3.34	4.12	6.56
ROME	a.	10.25	—	12.45	—	14.45	—	16.45	—	18.45	—	20.45	—	22.45	—	—	—	—	6.15	8.00	9.30

		ic	ic						ic				ic						
VENICE	p.	—	8.00	9.35	11.35	12.09	13.35	—	14.22	15.35	16.55	17.29	18.02	19.35	20.02	21.35	22.35	23.35	0.20
MESTRE	p.	6.04	8.12	9.48	11.48	12.19	13.48	14.23	14.32	15.48	17.06	17.39	18.14	19.48	20.14	21.48	22.48	23.48	0.31
BOLOGNA	a.	7.59	10.05	11.42	13.42	14.12	15.42	16.04	16.25	17.42	18.57	19.37	20.00	21.42	22.00	23.42	0.42	1.42	2.35

DIRECT NTERNATIONAL CARS

WLcc				ic ic EN WLcc			WLcc#
VENICE p.23.28	VENICE p. 13.05	VENICE p. 7.30 20.35 23.58	VENICE p. 17.51
MESTRE p. 23.40	LUGANO p. 19.14	MESTRE p. 7.42 12.47 20.46 1.05	MESTRE p. 18.02
GENOA a. 5.21	ZURICH p. 21.37	VIENNA a. 16.40 20.46 6.08 8.57	BASEL a. 2.40
NICE a. 11.17			

ec EN WL		EN		ec	
VENICE p. 14.05 20.10 22.02	VENICE p. 13.35	VENICE p. 12.05 22.02
MESTRE p. 14.17 20.22 22.42	MESTRE p. 13.46	MESTRE p. 12.17 22.42
LAUSANNE a. 21.11 5.55	VERONA a. 14.57	BERN a. 19.38
PARIS a. 8.25	MUNICH a. 21.02	GENEVA a. 19.48 6.36

Legend : c Milano Lambrate - d Florence Campo di Marte - ic Intercity - ec Eurocity - P Pendolino - WL Wagon Lits - EN Euronight - cc Cuccette - n only WL and cc - f Holidays - weekdays only, Florence Rifredi, not in August - not on the eve of holidays, Florence Rifredi - #Only Saturday and Sunday from Venice

DOMESTIC FLIGHTS

Freq.	Departures	Transfer	Arrivals	Flight
	VENICE			
D	6.45		7.30	AZ 1456L
D	9.30		10.15	AZ 600M
D	17.05		18.00	AZ 1452L
	L = Linate / M = Malpensa			
	VENICE	**NAPLES**	**PALERMO**	
D	7.10	8.20	9.50	AZ 1858
D	18.45	19.55	-	AZ 1250
	VENICE		**ROME**	
D	6.40		7.45	AZ 1468
D	7.35		8.40	AZ 1462
D	10.50		11.50	IG 1162
D	11.15		12.20	AZ 1470
D	14.45		15.50	AZ 1478
D	16.40		17.45	AZ 1476
D	19.15		20.20	AZ 1466
	VENICE		**TURIN**	
12345	7.25		8.35	EN 260

Freq.	Departures	Transfer	Arrivals	Flight
	MILAN		**VENICE**	
D	8.00		8.45	AZ 601M
D	15.45		16.40	AZ 1457L
D	22.00		22.45	AZ 1455L
	L = Linate / M = Malpensa			
	PALERMO	**NAPLES**	**VENICE**	
D	-	9.30	10.45	AZ 1251
D	18.40	19.35	21.40	AZ 1859
	ROME		**VENICE**	
D	8.45		9.50	IG 1161
D	9.05		10.10	AZ 1463
D	12.30		13.35	IG 1469
D	14.50		15.55	AZ 1471
D	17.20		18.25	AZ 1465
D	20.50		21.55	AZ 1461
D	22.20		23.25	AZ 1477
	TURIN		**VENICE**	
12345	13.35		14.45	EN 261

INTERNATIONAL FLIGHTS

Freq.	Departures	Transfer	Arrivals	Flight
	VENICE		**AMSTERDAM**	
D	11.45		13.45	KL 272
D	16.20		18.20	KL 274
	VENICE		**BARCELONA**	
12345	7.25	(Turin)	10.50	EN 260
D	12.25		14.15	SN 861
D	20.00		21.40	AZ 092
	VENICE		**BRUSSELS**	
123456	7.00		8.35	SN 838
D	15.25		17.00	SN 834
	VENICE		**COPENAGHEN**	
D	19.15		21.15	SK 692
	VENICE		**DÜSSELDORF**	
7	14.45		16.25	LH 3533
123456	14.45		16.25	LH 5367
	VENICE		**FRANKFURT**	
D	7.10		8.45	LH 3560
D	10.55		12.25	LH 3516
123457	14.20		15.55	LH 3534
D	18.35		20.10	LH 3562
	VENICE		**LONDON**	
D	10.00		11.05	AZ 272G
D	14.25		15.35	BA 589H
D	16.05		17.10	AZ 274G
		H = Heathrow / G = Gatwick		

Freq.	Departures	Transfer	Arrivals	Flight
	AMSTERDAM		**VENICE**	
D	9.05		10.55	KL 271
D	13.45		15.35	KL 273
	BARCELONA		**VENICE**	
D	8.30		10.10	AZ 093
12345	11.20	(Turin)	14.45	EN 261
D	13.00		14.40	SN 862
	BRUSSELS		**VENICE**	
D	10.00		11.35	SN 833
123456	19.05		20.40	SN 837
	COPENAGHEN		**VENICE**	
D	16.30		18.30	SK 691
	DÜSSELDORF		**VENICE**	
7	12.25		14.00	LH 3530
123456	12.45		14.15	LH 5324
	FRANKFURT		**VENICE**	
D	8.45		10.05	LH 3560
123457	12.20		13.35	LH 3516
D	16.30		17.50	LH 3534
D	21.40		23.00	LH 3562
	LONDON		**VENICE**	
D	10.15		13.20	BA 588H
D	12.00		15.00	AZ 295G
D	18.00		21.00	AZ4285G
		H = Heathrow / G = Gatwick		

Freq.	Departures	Transfer	Arrivals	Flight
	VENICE		**MADRID**	
D	11.45		16.40	AZ 094
	VENICE		**MONTPELLIER**	
14567	15.45		17.50	FU 123
	VENICE		**MOSCOW**	
7	9.00		14.10	SU 294
3	12.15		17.30	SU 294
	VENICE		**MUNICH**	
D	8.25		9.35	LH 6821
D	12.55		14.00	LH 6823
123457	17.00		18.10	LH 6825
	VENICE	(Milano)	**NY-NEWARK**	
D	9.30		14.20	AZ 600
	VENICE		**NICE**	
D	14.50		16.25	FU 605
	VENICE		**PARIS**	
123456	7.00		8.40	AF 635
D	9.00		10.40	AZ 370
D	13.30		15.10	AF 629
D	16.10		17.50	AZ 372
D	19.20		21.00	AF 627
	VENICE		**STÜTTGART**	
137	15.30		17.00	BA 3461
6	17.35		18.55	BA 3461
	VENICE		**VIENNA**	
D	7.20		8.45	VO 212
6	11.40		13.00	VO 214
123457	12.00		13.00	VO 214
123457	18.40		19.40	VO 216
6	19.00		20.20	VO 216
	VENICE	**LUGANO**	**ZÜRICH**	
123456	9.50	10.50	11.40	EN613/LX905
123457	15.35	16.35	17.55	EN615/LX913
123457	18.50	19.45	21.00	EN617/LX917

Freq.	Departures	Transfer	Arrivals	Flight
	MADRID		**VENICE**	
D	17.10		19.30	AZ 095
	MONTPELLIER		**VENICE**	
14567	10.50		12.45	FU 122
	MOSCOW		**VENICE**	
3	9.45		11.15	SU 293
6	18.55		20.15	SU 293
	MUNICH		**VENICE**	
D	11.15		12.25	LH 6822
D	15.15		16.25	LH 6824
123457	20.40		21.50	LH 6820
	NY-NEWARK	(Milano)	**VENICE**	
D	17.10		8.45	AZ 601
	NICE		**VENICE**	
D	12.40		14.00	FU 602
	PARIS		**VENICE**	
D	11.00		12.35	AF 658
D	12.15		13.35	AZ 371
D	16.35		18.10	AF 654
D	18.50		20.30	AZ 373
123457	19.50		21.25	AF 652
	STÜTTGART		**VENICE**	
137	13.35		15.05	BA 3460
6	15.45		17.05	BA 3460
	VIENNA		**VENICE**	
6	9.45		11.10	VO 213
123457	10.25		11.30	VO 213
D	17.10		18.10	VO 215
D	20.45		22.20	VO 217
	ZÜRICH	**LUGANO**	**VENICE**	
123456	7.15	8.00	9.20	LX900/EN612
12345	12.25	13.10	14.30	LX906/EN614
123457	16.00	16.45	18.20	LX912/EN616

LEGEND : AF = Air France - AZ = Alitalia - BA = British Airways and Deutsche BA -
EN = Air Dolomiti - NS = Eurowings - FU = Air Littoral - KL = Royal Dutch Airline - LG = Luxair -
LH = Lufthansa - LX = Cross Air - OS = Austrian Airlines - SK = SAS - Scandinavian Airlines -
SN = Sabena Airline - SU = Aeroflot - VO = Tyrol Airline - D = Daily - 1 = Monday - 2 = Tuesday -
3 = Wednesday - 4 = Thursday - 5 = Friday - 6 = Saturday - 7 = Sunday

Timetables are subject to change

Public transporation in Venice is based on vaporetti (water buses), motorboats and ferries. Taking a vaporetto, that stops at each imbarcadero or dock is equivalent to a tour of the heart of Venice. The timetables and schedules are posted at each imbarcadero. **Line 1** Accelerata is the most interesting for visitors, as it makes many stops along both sides of the Grand Canal, it runs from Piazzale Roma to the Lido.

MAIN WATER CONNECTIONS IN VENICE
From the automobile terminal at Tronchetto to the historic city center:
Line 82 via the Grand Canal (for the railroad station, Rialto, S. Marco) or via Canale della Giudecca (direct to S. Marco), in summer it continues to the Lido.
Line 3: summer line, morning service only to Rialto and S. Marco.

From Piazzale Roma, **Line 1**: makes all stops along the Grand Canal to the Lido, or **Line 82**.

From S. Marco to return to the railroad station, Piazzale Roma and Tronchetto, **Line 4** (summertime, afternoon service only), or **line 82**.

From Venice to the Lido, we suggest motorboat **Line 6** from the Paglia station (between S. Zaccaria and S. Marco); it departs every 20 minutes, the trip takes fifteen minutes.

The Lido can also be reached by car, using the ferry boat from Tronchetto (the trip takes about 35 minutes).

To go to Burano and Torcello: **Line 14** from S. Zaccaria (about 1 hour and 15 minutes), or **Line 12** from Fondamente Nove (about 45 minutes). **Line 52** goes to Fondamente Nove from Piazzale Roma or from the railroad station, and then continues to Murano.

From the Jesolo shore, it is best to reach Venice form Punta Sabbioni, where a motorboat takes about 45 minutes. Burano and Torcello can be reached by motorboat in a half hour.

The automobile terminal at Fusina is in service during the summer, with **Line 16** departures for Venice (Zattere) every half hour during the season.

Detailed and updated information and routes and schedules can be obtained form the Centro Informazioni ed Accoglienza della Azienda di Transporti ACTV in Piazzale Roma, open daily, including holidays, from 7:30 a.m. to 8:00 p.m. (phone 041-5287886 - fax 041-5222633).

It is advisable to purchase round-trip tickets, or special 24 hour, 3 or 7 day tickets.

Schedules are subject to change.

LINE 1 – Accelerato

(Line 1 stops are also numbered)

1. Piazzale Roma (Parisi) - nighttime service stops at S. Chiara
2. Railroad station (S. Lucia) - nighttime service stops at Scalzi
3. Riva di Biaso
4. S. Marcuola
5. S. Stae
6. Ca' d'Oro
7. Rialto
8. S. Silvestro
9. S. Angelo
10. S.Tomà
11. Ca' Rezzonico
12. Accademia
13. S. Maria del Giglio
14. S. Maria della Salute (commonly called "Salute")
15. S. Marco (Vallaresso)
16. S. Zaccaria (Danieli)
17. Arsenale
18. Giardini
19. S. Elena
20. Lido (S. Maria Elisabetta)

LINE 3 – Direct Tourist Service

(This is a summertime clockwise, circular service in summer)

Tronchetto "B"
Railroad (Scalzi)
Rialto
S. Samuele
Accademia
S. Marco (Giardinetti)

Via the Canale della Giudecca it goes to:
Tronchettto "B"

LINE 4 – Direct Tourist Service

(This is a summertime counter-clockwise, circular service)

Lido (S. Maria Elisabetta)
S. Zaccaria (Jolanda)
S. Marco (Giardinetti)
Acccademia
S. Samuele
Ferrovia (Scalzi)
P. Roma (S.Chiara)

Tronchetto "B" -
-Via the Canale della Giudecca it goes to:
S. Zaccaria (Jolanda)
Lido (S. Maria Elisabetta)

LINE 6 "Direct" (motorboat and ferry)

S. Zaccaria (Paglia)
Lido (S. Maria Ebisabetta)

LINE 10

S. Zaccaria (Monumento Vittorio Emanuele)
Grazia
S. Clemente

LINE 11

Ths is a special line that connects the Lido to Chioggia: the bus leaves from the Gran Viale on the Lido and goes south to Alberoni (Faro Rocchetta). The bus boards a ferryboat and goes as far as the Island of Pellestrina (S. Maria del Mare). The bus disembarks from the ferry and goes south, through the entire Island of Pellestrina to "Cimitero". Here the passengers board a motorboat that crosses the port to Chioggia. All arrivals and departures are correctly timed for proper connections.

LINE 12 - 14 - 14 barrato - Circular North Lagoon

This line is, also known as "Circolare Laguna Nord" and complements the vessels and schedules of Lines 12 (Venice - Burano - Torcello), 14 (Venice - Punta Sabbioni - Treporti - Burano) and 14 barrato (Venice - Punta Sabbioni). In summer it also connects with Line 6.
The entire route is the following:

S. Zaccaria (Paglia) - some seasonal runs depart from Pietà
Lido (S. Maria Elisabetta)
Lido (S. Nicolò) - only some runs in summer
Punta Sabbioni
Treporti
Burano
Torcello (not all runs include the Burano- Torcello ferry)
Mazzorbo
Murano (Faro)
Fondamente Nove

LINE 13

Fondamente Nove
Murano Faro
Vignole
S. Erasmo (Capannone)
S. Erasmo (Chiesa)
S. Erasmo (Punta Vela)
Treporti

LINE 16

(This is a summer route)

Fusina
Zattere (Traghetto)

LINE 20

S. Zaccaria (Monumento Vittorio Emanuele)
S. Servolo
S. Lazzaro

LINE 17 – (Car Ferry Boat)

Tronchetto
Lido (S. Nicolò)

in summer some runs are extended to Punta Sabbioni,
and the route becomes:

Tronchetto
Lido (S. Nicolò)
Punta Sabbioni

LINE 18

This is a summer route of little interest to visitors (last summer there were only 6 round-trip runs per day). It is shown for convenience, but it could be deleted from the guidebook.

Madonna dell'Orto
Fondamente Nove
Murano (Colonna)
Murano (Faro)
Murano (Navagero)
Murano (Museo)
S. Erasmo (Forte Massimiliano)
Lido (S. Nicolò)
Lido (S. Maria Elisabetta)

LINE 23

(This is a circular summer route)

S. Zaccaria (Jolanda)
S. Elena
Murano (Navagero)
Murano (Faro)
Murano (Colonna)
Cimitero
Fondamente Nove
Ospedale
Celestia
Tana
S. Zaccaria (Jolanda)

LINE 52 e 52 barrato – Direct

Lido (Casinò) - summer only
Lido (S. Maria Elisabetta)
S. Elena
Giardini (Biennale)
S. Zaccaria (Danieli)
Zattere (Ponte Lungo)
S. Marta
Piazzale Roma (Scomenzera)
Railroad (S. Lucia) - nighttime service stops at Scalzi
Ponte delle Guglie (known as "Guglie")
Ponte dei Tre Archi(known as "Tre Archi")
S. Alvise
Madonna dell'Orto
Fondamente Nove
Cimitero
Murano (Colonna)

As an alternative, the vessels continue to:
Murano (Serenella)
Murano (Venier)
Murano (Museo)

and return by the opposite route:
Murano (Faro)
Murano (Navagero)
Murano (Museo)

Line 52 barrato means there is a / on the number:

Piazzale Roma (Parisi)
Sacca Fisola
S. Eufemia
Zitelle
S.Zaccaria (Jolanda)
Tana
Celestia
Ospedale
Fondamente Nove
Cimitero
Murano (Colonna)
Murano (Serenella)
Murano (Venier)
Murano (Museo)
Murano (Navagero)
Murano (Faro)
Murano (Colonna)
The return journey makes the same stops in reverse order.

LINE 40

(This is a summer line)
It is also known as "Casinò Express".

Piazzale Roma (Parisi)
Tronchetto "B"
Lido (Casinò)

LINE 82 – *Vaporetto service*

S.Zaccaria (Monumento Vittorio Ernanuele)
S.Giorgio
Zitelle
Redentore
Giudecca (Traghetto)
S. Eufemia
Zattere (Traghetto)
S. Basilio
Sacca Fisola

At this point, some routes turn off for S. Marta and make their last stop (they are known as "82 verde" (green), the other are "82 rosso" (red) and continue (without stopping at S. Marta) for:
Tronchetto "B"
Piazzale Roma (S. Chiara)
Ferrovia (Scalzi)
S. Marcuola
Rialto
S.Tomà
S. Samuele
Accademia
S. Marco (Giardinetti)

from this point on, the line becomes seasonal. In summer it continues to:
S.Zaccaria (Jolanda)
Giardini (Biennale)
Lido (S. Maria Elisabetta)

- **Bacino Orseolo**
  ☎ 5289316
- **Calle Vallaresso**
  ☎ 5206120
- **Danieli** - (Riva Schiavoni)
  ☎ 5222254
- **Ferrovia** - (San Simon Piccolo)
  ☎ 718543
- **Isola Tronchetto**
  ☎ 5238919
- **Piazzale Roma**
  ☎ 5220581
- **Santa Maria del Giglio**
  ☎ 5222073
- **San Marco** - (molo)
  ☎ 5200685
- **Santa Sofia** - (Cannaregio)
  ☎ 5222844
- **San Tomà**
  ☎ 5205275
- **Trinità** - (Campo S. Moisé)
  ☎ 5231837
- **Rialto** - (Riva Carbon)
  ☎ 5224904

Lit. 80.000 for 50 minutes, up to six passengers.
Lit. 40.000 for every 20 minutes thereafter.
Rates for special services in excess of Lit. 80.000 are negotiable.
Lit. 100.000 for nighttime service between 8:00 p.m. and 8:00 a.m.

- **Radio Taxi**
  ☎ 5222303/723112
- **Ferrovia**
  ☎ 716286
- **Piazzale Roma** (Santa Chiara)
  ☎ 716922
- **Rialto**
  ☎ 5230575/723112
- **San Marco** (Molo)
  ☎ 5229750
- **Lido**
  ☎ 5260059
- **Aeroporto** (Marco Polo)
  Tel. 5415084
- **Coop. San Marco**
  ☎ 5222303/5235775
- **Coop. Veneziana**
  ☎ 716124

- **Coop. Serenissima**
  ☎ 5221265/5228538
- **Coop. Bucintoro**
  ☎ 723009
- **Coop. Fondamenta Nuove**
  ☎ 723009
- **Soc. Narduzzi & Solemar**
  ☎ 5200838/5231835
- **Soc. Marco Polo**
  ☎ 5300639
- **Soc. Sotoriva**
  ☎ 5237351
- **Soc. Serenissima**
  ☎ 5224281

BAGGAGE HANDLERS

 - **Accademia**
☎ 5224891

- **Bragora -** (Riva Schiavoni)
☎ 5287273

- **Castello -** (San Zaccaria)
☎ 5228901

- **Ferrovia**
☎ 715272

- **Piazzale Roma**
☎ 5203070/5223590

- **Rialto**
☎ 5205308

- **San Geremia**
☎ 715694

- **San Marco -**
(Orologio San Marco)
☎ 5232385

- **San Marco**
(Bacino Orseolo)
☎ 5200545

- **San Moisé**
☎ 5237578

- **Transbagagli Ferrovia**
☎ 715272

- **Transbagagli Piazzale Roma**
☎ 5223590

- **Vallaresso -**
(cl. Vallaresso)
☎ 5224412

Public Transportation

Piazzale Roma
☎ 5287886

Trains:

Stazione Santa Lucia e
Stazione di Mestre
☎ 715555

Airlines:

Aeroporto Marco Polo
☎ 661262

Taxis:

Radio Taxi
☎ 936222

Bycicle rental:

Bruno Lazzari

Gran viale Santa Maria Elisabetta,
Lido, 21b
☎ 5268019

Giorgio Barbieri

Via Zara, Lido 5
☎ 5261490

Garages

Venezia, Isola del Tronchetto
☎ 5207555
Venezia, P.le Roma Garage Comunale
☎ 5222308
Venezia, P.le Roma Garage S. Marco
☎ 5232213

Parking

Venezia, Isola del Tronchetto
☎ 5207555
Venezia, P.le Roma ACI
☎ 5206235
Punta Sabbioni
Treporti Ricevitoria

Tourist Board (I.A.T.)

Venezia S. Marco
☎ 5226356
Lido, Viale S. M Elisabetta
☎ 52665721
Marghera, Rotatoria autostradale
☎ e Fax 937764
Cà Savio, via Fausta, 79/G
☎ e Fax 966010
Dolo - Arino Sud, Autostrada Padova
- Venezia
☎ 413945

- Gallerie dell'Accademia
Accademia - Dorsoduro - weekdays and holidays 9/19   ☎ 5222247
- Palazzo Ducale
Piazzetta San Marco - weekdays and holidays 9/17   ☎ 5224951
- Collezione Peggy Guggenheim
S. Gregorio, 701 - Dorsoduro - (closed Tuesdays)
weekdays and holidays 11/18   ☎ 5206288
- Museo Civico Correr
Piazza San Marco - (closed Tuesdays) weekdays and holidays 10/16   ☎ 5225625
- Museo d'Arte Moderna Ca' Pesaro
San Stae, S. Cróce - (closed Mondays) weekdays and holidays 10/16   ☎ 721127
- Museo Fortuny
San Beneto, 3780 San Marco   ☎ 5200995
- Museo del Settecento Veneziano
Ca' Rezzonico (San Barnaba) - (closed Fridays)
weekdays and holidays10/16   ☎ 2410100
- Museo di Storia Naturale
S.Croce, 1730 - (closed on holidays) weekdays and holidays 9/13   ☎ 5240885
- Museo Storico Navale
Arsenale, 2148 Castello - (closed on holidays) weekdays 9/13   ☎ 5200276
- Ca' d'Oro
Galleria Franchetti, Cannaregio - weekdays and holidays 9/14   ☎ 5238790
- Museo Archeologico
Piazza San Marco, 52 - weekdays and holidays 9/14   ☎ 5225978
- Museo Orientale
Ca' Pesaro (San Stae) - (closed Mondays) - weekdays and holidays 9/14 ☎ 5241173
- Galleria di Palazzo Cini
S. Vio, Dorsoduro, 864 (closed in winter)   ☎ 5210755
- Museo Dipinti Sacri Bizantini
Istituto Ellenico, Ponte dei Greci, Castello, 3412 - weekdays 9/13 e14/17☎ 5226581
- Palazzo Mocenigo
San Stae, 1992 - (closed on holidays) weekdays 8.30/13.30   ☎ 721798
- Museo Diocesano
Ponte della Canonica - (closed on Sundays)
weekdays and holidays 10.30/12.30   ☎ 5229166
- Museo Comunità Ebraica
Cannaregio, 2902/b (closed on Saturdays)
weekdays and holidays 10/16.30   ☎ 715359
- Archivio Storico delle Arti Contemporanee
Santa Croce, 2214 - (closed on Sundays) weekdays 9/13   ☎ 5218711
- Monastero Mekhitarista
Isola San Lazzaro degli Armeni - weekdays and holidays 15/20   ☎ 5260104

- **Archivio di Stato**
  San Polo, 3002   ☎ 5222281
- **Biblioteca Marciana**
  Piazzetta San Marco - weekdays 9/19 and Saturdays 9/13.30   ☎ 5208788
- **Museo Fondazione Scientifica Querini Stampalia**
  Castello, 4778 - (closed Mondays)   ☎ 5225235
- **Casa Goldoni**
  San Tomà, San Polo - (closed on holidays) - weekdays 8/13.30   ☎ 5236353
- **Scuola Grande di San Rocco**
  Campo San Rocco, Frari - weekdays and holidays 10/16   ☎ 5234864
- **Scuola di San Giorgio degli Schiavoni**
  Ponte dei Greci, Castello (closed Mondays)   ☎ 5228828
- **Scuola dei Carmini**
  Carmini, Dorsoduro (closed Sundays) - weekdays and holidays 9/18 ☎ 5289420
- **Palazzo Labia - Salone del Tiepolo**
  San Geremia, Cannaregio   ☎ 5242812
- **Galleria Basilica di San Marco**
  Piazza San Marco - weekdays and holidays 9.30/16.30   ☎ 5225205
- **Pala d'Oro e Tesoro**
  Basilica San Marco - weekdays 9.30/16.30 and holidays 14/16.30   ☎ 5225697
- **Campanile di San Marco**
  Piazza San Marco - weekdays and holidays 9.30/16   ☎ 5224064
- **Campanile San Giorgio**
  Isola di San Giorgio - weekdays and holidays 9.30/17   ☎ 5289900
- **Torre dell'Orologio**
  Mercerie, San Marco   ☎ 5231879
- **Basilica dei Frari**
  Campo dei Frari, San Polo   ☎ 5222637
- **Museo Vetrario di Murano**
  Isola di Murano (closed Wednesdays) - weekdays and holidays 10/16 ☎ 739586
- **Scuola di Merletti di Burano**
  Piazza Galuppi, Isola di Burano (closed Mondays)   ☎ 730034
- **Museo dell'Estuario di Torcello**
  Palazzo del Consiglio, Torcello (closed Mondays and holidays)   ☎ 730761
- **Cattedrale di Torcello**
  Isola di Torcello   ☎ 730084
- **Convento di San Francesco del Deserto**
  San Francesco del Deserto - weekdays and holidays 9/11 e15/17   ☎ 5286863
- **Aquarium**
  Calle Albanesi   ☎ 5207770

BANKS

- **BANCA COMMERCIALE ITALIANA**
  Via XXII Marzo 2188 ☎ 5296811
- **BANCA DEL FRIULI**
  San Marco 4586, Campo San Luca ☎ 5285744
- **BANCA D'ITALIA**
  San Marco 4799 ☎ 2709111
- **BANCA DI ROMA**
  Mercerie dell'Orologio 191 ☎ 662411
- **BANCA NAZIONALE DEL LAVORO**
  Bacino Orseolo ☎ 667511
- **BANCA NAZ. DELLE COMUNICAZIONI**
  Rio Terrà San Leonardo 1353 ☎ 717722
- **BANCA POPOLARE DI NOVARA**
  San Marco 4187 San Luca ☎ 5231640
- **BANCA POPOLARE DI VERONA**
  San Marco 1336 ☎ 5205344
- **BANCO AMBROSIANO VENETO**
  San Marco 4481 - Calle Goldoni ☎ 2903111
- **BANCO DI NAPOLI**
  Campo San Gallo 1122 - Bacino Orseolo ☎ 5209855
- **BANCO DI SICILIA**
  San Marco 5051, via 2 Aprile ☎ 5220525
- **BANCO SAN MARCO**
  San Marco 383 ☎ 5293711
- **CASSA DI RISPARMIO DI VENEZIA**
  San Marco 4216 Campo Manin ☎ 5291111
- **CASSA DI RISPARMIO DELLE PROVINCE LOMBARDE**
  San Marco 1126 Bacino Orseolo ☎ 5330411
- **CREDITO ITALIANO**
  Campo San Salvador ☎ 5226330
- **DEUTSCHE BANK**
  Via XXII Marzo 2216/17 ☎ 5490811
- **IST. FEDERALE CASSE RISPARMIO**
  San Vidal 2847 ☎ 5205111
- **ISTITUTO MOBILIARE ITALIANO**
  Dorsoduro 1057 San Trovaso ☎ 5229403
- **MEDIOCREDITO DELLE VENEZIE**
  Cannaregio 3935 ☎ 5218444
- **MONTE DEI PASCHI DI SIENA**
  Santa Croce 574 ☎ 5204000

CONSULATES

- **AUSTRIA**
  Santa Croce 252
  ☎ 5240556

- **BELGIUM**
  San Marco 1470
  ☎ 5224124

- **BRAZIL**
  Campo S. Luca 4580/A
  ☎ 5204131

- **CHILE**
  San Marco 286
  ☎ 5202442

- **CZECH REPUBLIC**
  San Marco 1583/A
  ☎ 5210383

- **DENMARK**
  San Marco 4020
  ☎ 5200822

- **FINLAND**
  San Giuliano - Mestre
  ☎ 5319066

- **FRANCE**
  Dorsoduro 1397
  ☎ 5222392

- **GERMANY**
  Cannaregio 4201
  ☎ 5237675

- **GREAT BRITAIN**
  Dorsoduro 1051
  ☎ 5227207

- **GREECE**
  San Polo, Rialto 720
  ☎ 5237260

- **HUNGARY**
  San Marco 286
  ☎ 5239408

- **LIBERIA**
  V. Istria - Lido
  ☎ 5265878

- **LUXEMBOURG**
  Castello 5312
  ☎ 5222047

- **MALTA**
  Santa Croce 515
  ☎ 5222644

- **MEXICO**
  San Marco 286
  ☎ 5237445

- **NETHERLANDS**
  San Marco 423
  ☎ 5283416

- **NORWAY**
  Rotonda Garibaldi
  12/7 - Mestre
  ☎ 5340447

- **PANAMA**
  Santa Maria Elisabetta
  8/A - Lido
  ☎ 5267169

- **PORTUGAL**
  San Marco 1253
  ☎ 5223446

- **REPUBLIC OF SAN MARINO**
  San Marco 5017/A
  ☎ 5228239

- **REPUBLIC OF SOUTH AFRICA**
  Santa Croce 464
  ☎ 5241599

- **SWEDEN**
  c/o LIGABUE s.p.a.
  Piazzale Roma -
  Santa Croce 499
  ☎ 2705611

- **SWITZERLAND**
  Dorsoduro 810
  ☎ 5225996

- **TURKEY**
  San Marco 2414
  ☎ 5230707

- **UNITED STATES OF AMERICA**
  Largo Donegani 1, Milano
  ☎ 02/290351

- Basilica di **S. MARCO,** Piazza San Marco   ☎ 5225697
  7.00 - 8.00 - 9.00 -10.00 (High Mass in Latin) -11.30 -12.30 -18.45
  Feriali 7.00 - 7.30 - 8.00 - 9.00 -10.00 -11.00 -12.00 -18.45
- Chiesa di **S. MOISE',** Campo San Moisé, San Marco   ☎ 5285840
  (19.00) - 9.00 -11.00 -12.00 -19.00
- Chiesa di **S. SALVADOR,** Campo San Salvador, San Marco   ☎ 5236717
  (18.30) -10.00 -11.30 -18.30
-Chiesa di **S. STEFANO,** Campo Santo Stefano 3825   ☎ 5222362
  (19.00) - 8.00 -10.00 -11.30 - 19.00
-Basilica di **SS. GIOVANNI E PAOLO,** Campo San Giovanni e Paolo 6363   ☎ 5237510
  (18.30) - 8.00 -10.30 -12.00 -18.30
- Basilica di **S. MARIA FORMOSA,** Campo Santa Maria Formosa   ☎ 5234645
  (18.30) - 9.00 -10.00 -11.30 -18.30
- Chiesa di **SANTA MARIA DI NAZARETH** (Scalzi), Ferrovia - Cannaregio
  (18.30) - 8.00 - 9.30 -10.30 -11.30 -18.00
- Chiesa di **S. ZACCARIA,** Campo San Zaccaria 4693 - Castello   ☎ 5221257
  (18.30) -10.00 -1200 -18.30
- Chiesa di **S. NICOLA** (dei Tolentini), Campo dei Tolentini 265   ☎ 5225806
  (18.30) - 9.00 -10.30 -12.00 -18.30
- Basilica di **S. MARIA GLORIOSA DEI FRARI,** Campo dei Frari 3072   ☎ 5222637
  (18.30) -10.30 -1200 -18.30
- Chiesa dei **GESUATI,** Zattere - Dorsoduro   ☎ 5230625
  (18.30) - 8.00 -10.00 -1200 -18.30
- Chiesa di **S. ZULIAN,** Campo San Zulian - S. Marco   ☎ 5235383
  11.00 -19.30
- Chiesa di **S. MARIA DELLA SALUTE** (Madonna della Salute)   ☎ 5225558
  9.00 -11.00
- Chiesa del **SS. REDENTORE,** Giudecca 195   ☎ 5231415
  (18.30) - 8.00 -10.00 -18.30
- Chiesa di **S. GIORGIO MAGGIORE,** Isola di San Giorgio Maggiore   ☎ 5289900
  8.30 -11.00 (Gregorian chant Mass)
- Chiesa di **S. MARIA ASSUNTA,** Isola di Torcello   ☎ 730084
  (16.30) - 9.30
- Chiesa di **S. M. ELISABETTA - LIDO,** Riviera Santa Maria Elisabetta   ☎ 5260072
  (18.30)- 8.00 -10.00 -11.00 -1200 -18.30
- Chiesa di **S. ANTONIO DA PADOVA - LIDO,** Piazza Sant'Antonio   ☎ 5261386
  (18.30) - 8.00 - 9.30 -11.00 -18.30
- Chiesa di **SANT'IGNAZIO DI LOYOLA,** Piazzale Gamba - Cà Bianca Lido   ☎ 5261480
  (18.30) - 8.00 - 9.30 - 11.30 - 18.00

- **ACCADEMIA STUMENTALE DI VENEZIA**
  Santa Croce, 2239 ☎ 5240627
- **AGENZIA MUSICALE VENEZIA CLASSIC Srl**
  San Marco, 213 ☎ 5223961
- **AMICI DEI MUSEI**
  Piazza San Marco, 63 ☎ 5210155
- **ASSOCIAZIONE CULTURALE ITALO-TEDESCA**
  Cannaregio, 4118 ☎ 5245275
- **ATENEO VENETO**
  Campo San Fantin, 1897 ☎ 5224459
- **ASS.VENEZIANA ALBERGATORI (A.V.A.)**
  Cannaregio, 3829 ☎ 5228004
- **BIENNALE DI VENEZIA**
  San Marco (Palazzo Giustinian) ☎ 5236488
- **CENTRO COORDINAMENTO CULTURALE**
  Via Forte Gazzera, 11 - Mestre ☎ 917257
- **CENTRO DI CULTURA DI PALAZZO GRASSI**
  Campo San Samuele ☎ 5231680
- **COMUNITÀ DEI PORTI ADRIATICI**
  San Marco, 1093 ☎ 5237940
- **FONDAZIONE CINI**
  Isola di San Giorgio Maggiore ☎ 5289900
- **FONDAZIONE GUGGENHEIM**
  San Gregorio, Dorsoduro, 701 ☎ 5206288
- **FONDAZIONE LEVI**
  San Marco, 2893 ☎ 786711
- **FOND. SCIENTIFICA QUERINI STAMPALIA**
  Castello, 4778 ☎ 5225235
- **ISTITUTO ELLENICO DI STUDI**
  Castello, 3412 ☎ 5226581
- **IST. INTERN. PER LA RICERCA TEATRALE**
  San Tomà (Casa Goldoni), 2794 ☎ 5236353
- **IST. VENETO DI SCIENZE - LETTERE - ARTI**
  Campo Santo Stefano, 2945 ☎ 5210177
- **LA CONCERTANTE DI VENEZIA**
  uff. prom. Via Tergolina, 6 - Mestre ☎ 984997
- **VENEZIA MUSICA ASS. INTERNAZIONALE**
  Campiello dei Miracoli, 6075/A

PUBS AND PIANO BARS

- *ANTICO MARTINI E MARTINI SCALA*
  Restaurant with piano bar
  Campo San Fantin, 1983
  ☎ 5224121

- *LE BISTROT DE VENISE*
  Restaurant with cabaret, music and poetry
  Calle dei Fabbri - San Marco 4685
  ☎ 5236651

- *DEVIL'S FOREST PUB*
  Original music
  Campo San Bartolomeo - Rialto
  ☎ 5236651

- *LINEA D'OMBRA*
  Restaurant with live music
  Punta della Dogana - Zattere 12
  ☎ 5285259

- *IL PARADISO PERDUTO*
  Restaurant with music
  Cannaregio, 2540
  ☎ 750581

- *THE FIDDLER'S ELBOW IRISH PUB*
  Cannaregio, 3847
  ☎ 5239930

THEATERS AND CINEMAS

- LA FENICE
S. Fantin 2549
☎ 5210161

- GOLDONI
Calle Goldoni
☎ 5205422

- DEL RIDOTTO
Calle Vallaresso
☎ 5222939

- A L'AVOGARIA
Dorsoduro 1617
☎ 5206130

- FONDAMENTA NUOVE
Cannaregio 5013
☎ 5224498

- CORSO
Mestre
☎ 972615

- TONIOLO
Mestre
☎ 971666

- ACCADEMIA
Dorsoduro 1019
☎ 5287706

- CENTRALE
S. Marco 1659
☎ 5228201

- OLIMPIA
S. Marco 1094
☎ 5205439

- RITZ
S. Marco 617
☎ 5204429

- ASTRA
Via Corfù - Lido
☎ 5260289

VENICE BY NIGHT

CASINOS

- Casinò Municipale di Venezia
Palazzo Vendramin Calergi,
Cannaregio - San Marcuola
(in winter)
☎ 5297111
- Lido - Lungomare Marconi
(in summer)
☎ 5297111

DISCOTHEQUES:

- CLUB EL SOUK Discoteca
Accademia 1056/a
☎ 5200371

- ACROPOLIS Discoteca
Lungomare Marconi, 22
Lido di Venezia ☎ 5260466

CLUBS

- **ACCADEMIA ITALIANA DELLA CUCINA**
  Via Emo, 4 - Lido   ☎ 5260474
- **AEROCLUB ANCILLOTTO**
  Aeroporto Nicelli - San Nicolò Lido   ☎ 5260808
- **AI MIRACOLI CLUB**
  Musica classica, bar - Campiello Miracoli 6075   ☎ 5230616
- **ASSOCIAZIONE VELICA LIDO (A.V.L.)**
  Terre Perse Malamocco - Lido   ☎ 770648
- **AMICI DELLA RILEGATURA D'ARTE**
  c/o Fondazione Querini Stampalia - Castello 4778   ☎ 5225235
- **BACKGAMMON CLUB VENEZIA**
  c/o Antica Osteria Codroma Dorsoduro 2540   ☎ 5204161
- **CIRCOLO BRIDGE DI VENEZIA**
  Campo Santa Maria del Giglio 2473   ☎ 5225337
- **CIRCOLO GOLF VENEZIANO**
  Via del Forte Alberoni - Lido   ☎ 731015
- **CIRCOLO IPPICO VENEZIANO**
  Ca' Bianca - Lido   ☎ 5261820
- **CIRCOLO MOTONAUTICO VENEZIANO**
  San Marco 1365   ☎ 5222692
- **CLUB DELL'OSPITE**
  S. Elena, V.le Piave 18/a   ☎ 5231457
- **DIPORTO VELICO VENEZIANO (D.V.V.)**
  Sant'Elena   ☎ 5231927
- **LIONS CLUB - LIDO**
  c/o Hotel Villa Mabapa - Lido di Venezia   ☎ 5260590
- **LIONS CLUB - VENEZIA**
  Hotel Europa & Regina - Venezia   ☎ 5200477
- **ROTARY CLUB**
  (Segreteria) San Marco 4391   ☎ 5229112
- **PANATHLON CLUB**
  Venezia   ☎ 5210266
- **SAN GIORGIO GLI SPORT DELL'ACQUA**
  Associazione sportiva - Castello 1369   ☎ 5201073
- **SPORTCENTER LIDO**
  Eurotel - Lungomare Marconi - Lido di Venezia   ☎ 5268797
- **SPORTING CLUB VENEZIA**
  Lido via Malamocco (loc. Bassanello)   ☎ 770801
- **THE INTERNATIONAL PROPELLER CLUB**
  S. Marco 1093   ☎ 5237940
- **ZONTA CLUB INTERNATIONAL**
  c/o Hotel Bel Sito   ☎ 5228400

EMERGENCY PHONE NUMBERS

- **ACI** (Automobile Club - road service)   ☎   116
- **AIRPORT** - Information   ☎ 2609260
- **AIRPORT** - Lost & Found   ☎ 2606436
- **AMBULANCE** - Venice   ☎ 5230000
- **AMBULANCE** - Mestre   ☎ 988988
- **ASSOCIAZIONE VOLONTARI DEL SOCCORSO** (volunteer ambulance) ☎ 914186
- **CARABINIERI EMERGENCY**   ☎   112
- **CARABINIERI** - Piazzale Roma   ☎ 5235333
- **CITY HALL**   ☎ 2708111
- **CUSTOMS** - Mestre   ☎ 984877
- **CUSTOMS** - Tessera Airport   ☎ 5415991
- **DOCTOR'S OFFICE** - Lido   ☎ 5261750
- **FIRE DEPARTMENT** - Venice   ☎ 5200222
- **FIRE DEPARTMENT** - Mestre   ☎ 5020288
- **FIRE DEPARTMENT** - Lido   ☎ 5260222
- **HARBOR OFFICE**   ☎ 5205600
- **HIGHWAY POLICE** - Mestre   ☎ 5343232
- **ITALIAN STATE RAILWAYS** - Information   ☎ 715555
- **ITALIAN STATE RAILWAYS** - Lost & Found   ☎ 785238
- **MARCO POLO AIRPORT**   ☎ 2606111
- **MUNICIPAL POLICE** - Venice   ☎ 2708203
- **MUNICIPAL POLICE** - Piazzale Roma/Tronchetto   ☎ 5222612
- **MUNICIPAL POLICE** - Mestre   ☎ 985855
- **MUNICIPAL POLICE** - Lido   ☎ 5260395
- **POLICE EMERGENCY**   ☎   113
- **POLICE** (FLYING SQUAD) - Venice   ☎   113
- **POLICE** - Santa Chiara   ☎ 5284666
- **POLICE** (FLYING SQUAD) - Mestre   ☎ 981400
- **POLICE HEADQUARTERS AND PASSPORT OFFICE**   ☎ 2703511
- **TOURIST INFORMATION OFFICE**   ☎ 5226356

✱✱✱✱✱ L

- **CIPRIANI**
  Giudecca 10 (central location)   ☎ 5207744
- **DANIELI**
  Riva degli Schiavoni 4196 (panoramic)   ☎ 5226480
- **GRITTI PALACE**
  San Marco 2467   ☎ 794611

✱✱✱✱

- **AMADEUS**
  Lista di Spagna 227 (central location)   ☎ 715300
- **BAUER GRUNWALD E GRAND HOTEL**
  San Marco 1459 - Campo San Moisé   ☎ 5207022
- **BELLINI**
  Cannaregio 116 (central location)   ☎ 715095
- **CARLTON EXECUTIVE**
  Santa Croce 578 (central location)   ☎ 718488
- **CAVALLETTO & DOGE ORSEOLO**
  San Marco 1107 (central location)   ☎ 5200955
- **CONCORDIA**
  Calle Larga - San Marco 367   ☎ 5206866
- **EUROPA & REGINA**
  San Marco 2159   ☎ 5200477
- **GABRIELLI SANDWIRTH**
  Riva degli Schiavoni 4110   ☎ 5231580
- **LONDRA PALACE**
  Riva degli Schiavoni 4171 (central location)   ☎ 5200533
- **LUNA HOTEL BAGLIONI**
  San Marco 1243 (central location)   ☎ 5289840
- **METROPOLE**
  Riva degli Schiavoni 4149 (central location)   ☎ 5205044
- **MONACO & GRAND CANAL**
  San Marco 1325   ☎ 5200211
- **PALAZZO DEL GIGLIO**
  San Marco 2462   ☎ 5205166
- **PRINCIPE**
  Lista di Spagna 146/7 (central location)   ☎ 715022
- **SOFITEL**
  Santa Croce 245 (central location)   ☎ 710400
- **STAR HOTEL SPLENDID SUISSE**
  Mercerie 760   ☎ 5200755

HOTELS IN VENICE

***

- ABBAZIA
Calle Priuli, 68 - Cannaregio (100m from Railway Station)   ☎ 717333

- ACCADEMIA VILLA MARAVEGE
Dorsoduro 1058 (central location)   ☎ 5210188

- AL SOLE
Santa Croce 136 (central location)   ☎ 5232144

- AMERICAN
San Vio - Accademia 628 (central location)   ☎ 5204733

- ATENEO
San Marco 1876 (central location)   ☎ 5200777

- BASILEA
Santa Croce 817 (central location)   ☎ 718477

- BONVECCHIATI
Calle Goldoni 4488 - San Marco (central location)   ☎ 5285017

- CARPACCIO
San Polo 2765 (on Canal Grande)   ☎ 5235946

- CASTELLO
Castello 4365 (central location)   ☎ 5230217

- DO POZZI
San Marco 2347 (central location)   ☎ 5207855

- FIRENZE
San Marco 1490 (central location)   ☎ 5222858

- GARDENA
Santa Croce 239 (central location)   ☎ 5235549

- KETTE
San Moisé 2053 - San Marco (central location)   ☎ 5207766

- LA FENICE ET DES ARTISTES
San Marco 1936 (central location)   ☎ 5232333

- MARCONI
San Polo Riva del Vin 729 (central location)   ☎ 5222068

- NAZIONALE
Cannaregio 158 (central location)   ☎ 716133

- OLIMPIA
Santa Croce 395 (central location)   ☎ 5226141

- PANADA
Calle degli Specchieri 656 - San Marco   ☎ 5209088

- PICCOLA FENICE
San Marco 3614   ☎ 5204909

- SAN MOISE'
San Marco 2058 (central location)   ☎ 5203755

- SCANDINAVIA
Castello 5240 (central location)   ☎ 5223507

HOTELS IN VENICE

★★

- **AI DUE FANALI**
  Santa Croce 946 (central location)   ☎ 718490
- **ATLANTICO**
  Calle dei Rimedi 4416 - Castello   ☎ 5209244
- **CAMPIELLO**
  San Zaccaria 4647 (central location)   ☎ 5205764
- **CASA FONTANA**
  Campo San Zaccaria 4701 - Castello (central location)   ☎ 5220579
- **DOLOMITI**
  Calle Priuli 73   ☎ 715113
- **FALIER**
  Salizzada S. Pantalon 130 (central location)   ☎ 710882
- **GALLINI**
  Calle della Verona 3673 - San Marco   ☎ 5204515
- **GORIZIA**
  Calle dei Fabbri 4696/A (central location)   ☎ 5223737
- **HESPERIA**
  Cannaregio 459 (central location)   ☎ 715251
- **LA CALCINA**
  Dorsoduro 780 (central location)   ☎ 5206466
- **LA FORCOLA**
  Cannaregio 2356 (50m from Casinò)   ☎ 5241484
- **LISBONA**
  San Marco 2153 (central location)   ☎ 5286774
- **MESSNER**
  Dorsoduro 216 (central location)   ☎ 5227443
- **MIGNON**
  Cannaregio 4535 (central location)   ☎ 5237388
- **ORION**
  San Marco Spadaria 700/A (central location)   ☎ 5223053
- **PAGANELLI**
  Riva degli Schiavoni 4182 (central location)   ☎ 5224324
- **SAN ZULIAN**
  San Marco 535 (central location)   ☎ 5225872
- **SERENISSIMA**
  Calle Goldoni - San Marco 4486 (central location)   ☎ 5200011
- **STELLA ALPINA EDELWEISS**
  Calle Priuli - Cannaregio 99/D (central location)   ☎ 715179
- **TROVATORE**
  Calle delle Rasse 4534 (central location)   ☎ 5224611

✶

- AL GALLO
Santa Croce 197/G (central location)   ☎ 5236761
- AL GAZZETTINO
San Marco 4971 (central location)   ☎ 5286523
- ANTICO CAPON
Dorsoduro 3004/B (central location)   ☎ 5285292
- BRIDGE
Castello 4498 (central location)   ☎ 5205287
- BUDAPEST
San Marco 2143   ☎ 5220514
- CASA BOCCASSINI
Cannaregio 5295   ☎ 5229892
- CASA PERON
Salizzada San Pantalon 85 (central location)   ☎ 711038
- CORONA
Castello 4464   ☎ 5229174
- DA PINO
Dorsoduro 3941 (central location)   ☎ 5223646
- DONI
Castello S. Zaccaria 4656 (at S. Marco)   ☎ 5224267
- GALLERIA
Accademia 878/A   ☎ 5204172
- LOCANDA FIORITA
San Marco 3457/A (central location)   ☎ 5234754
- MINERVA E NETTUNO
Lista di Spagna 230   ☎ 715968
- PIAVE
Castello 4838/40 (central location)   ☎ 5285174
- RIVA
Castello Ponte dell'Angelo 5310   ☎ 5227034
- SAN GEREMIA
Cannaregio 290/A (central location)   ☎ 716260
- SAN SALVADOR
Calle Galiazzo 5264   ☎ 5289147
- SANTA LUCIA
Cannaregio 358   ☎ 715180
- TIEPOLO
Castello 4510   ☎ 5231315
- VILLA ROSA
Calle della Misericordia 389 - Cannaregio   ☎ 716569

RESTAURANTS IN VENICE

- **A LA VALIGIA**
  Calle dei Fabbri 4697 (historical center)
  Typical setting - home cooking ☎ 5223737
- **A LA VECIA CAVANA**
  SS. Apostoli 4624 - Cannaregio (historical center)
  Family setting - typical cuisine ☎ 5287106
- **AGLI ALBORETTI**
  Dorsoduro 882 (historical center)
  Elegant setting - refined cuisine ☎ 5230058
- **AL CAMPIELLO**
  Calle dei Fuseri 4346 - (historical center)
  Elegant setting - refined cuisine ☎ 5206396
- **AL CONTE PESCAOR**
  San Marco 544 - (historical center)
  Typical setting - local cuisine ☎ 5221483
- **AL GIARDINETTO**
  Castello 2375 (historical center)
  Typical setting - local cuisine ☎ 5285332
- **ANTICO MARTINI**
  San Marco 1983 - (near Teatro La Fenice)
  Elegant setting - refined cuisine ☎ 5224121
- **CANOVA**
  San Marco 1243 (historical center)
  Elegant setting - refined cuisine ☎ 5209550
- **DA CRECOLA**
  Santa Croce 1459 (historical center)
  Family setting - home cooking ☎ 5241496
- **DO LEONI**
  Riva degli Schiavoni 4171 (historical center)
  Elegant setting - local cuisine ☎ 5200533
- **GRAN CAFFE' QUADRI**
  Piazza San Marco 120
  Elegant setting - refined cuisine ☎ 5222105
- **HOSTARIA DA FRANZ**
  Castello 754
  Typical setting - local cuisine ☎ 5227505
- **IL CORTILE**
  Calle XXII Marzo 2398
  Elegant setting - local cuisine ☎ 5208938
- **LA TERRAZZA**
  Riva degli Schiavoni 4196 (panoramic)
  Elegant setting - local cuisine ☎ 5226480
- **LES DEUX LION**
  Riva degli Schiavoni 4171 (historical center)
  Refined cuisine ☎ 5220533

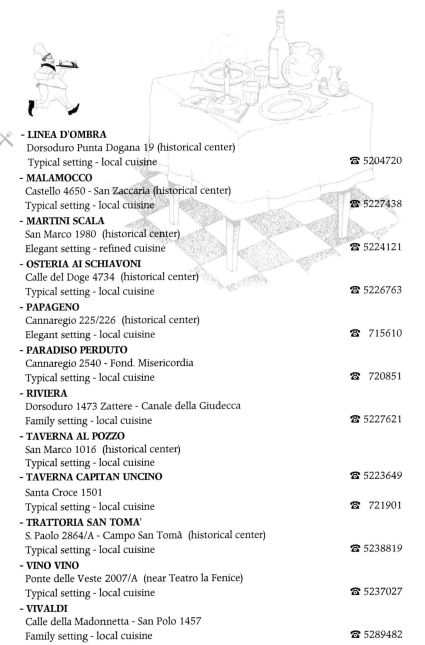

- LINEA D'OMBRA
Dorsoduro Punta Dogana 19 (historical center)
Typical setting - local cuisine ☎ 5204720

- MALAMOCCO
Castello 4650 - San Zaccaria (historical center)
Typical setting - local cuisine ☎ 5227438

- MARTINI SCALA
San Marco 1980 (historical center)
Elegant setting - refined cuisine ☎ 5224121

- OSTERIA AI SCHIAVONI
Calle del Doge 4734 (historical center)
Typical setting - local cuisine ☎ 5226763

- PAPAGENO
Cannaregio 225/226 (historical center)
Elegant setting - local cuisine ☎ 715610

- PARADISO PERDUTO
Cannaregio 2540 - Fond. Misericordia
Typical setting - local cuisine ☎ 720851

- RIVIERA
Dorsoduro 1473 Zattere - Canale della Giudecca
Family setting - local cuisine ☎ 5227621

- TAVERNA AL POZZO
San Marco 1016 (historical center)
Typical setting - local cuisine
- TAVERNA CAPITAN UNCINO ☎ 5223649
Santa Croce 1501
Typical setting - local cuisine ☎ 721901

- TRATTORIA SAN TOMA'
S. Paolo 2864/A - Campo San Tomà (historical center)
Typical setting - local cuisine ☎ 5238819

- VINO VINO
Ponte delle Veste 2007/A (near Teatro la Fenice)
Typical setting - local cuisine ☎ 5237027

- VIVALDI
Calle della Madonnetta - San Polo 1457
Family setting - local cuisine ☎ 5289482

★★★★★ L

- EXCELSIOR
Lungomare Marconi 41 ☎ 5260201

★★★★

- BIASUTTI
Via E. Dandolo 29 - (300 m. from the sea) ☎ 5260120
- DES BAINS CIGA HOTEL
Lungomare Marconi 17 - (panoramic location) ☎ 5265921
- GOLF
Stada del Forte 1- Malamocco - (20 m. from the sea) ☎ 5269512
- LE BOULEVARD
Via Gran Viale 41 - (200 m. from the sea) ☎ 5261990
- VILLA MABAPA
Riviera San Nicolò 16 - (panoramic location) ☎ 5260590

★★★

- ATLANTA AUGUSTUS
Via Lepanto 15 - (100 m. from San Marco vaporetto stop) ☎ 5261205
- BELVEDERE
Piazzale Santa Maria Elisabetta 4 ☎ 5260115
- BUON PESCE
Riviera San Nicolò 50 - (near the sea) ☎ 5268599
- HELVETIA
Via Gran Viale S. M. Elisabetta - (50 m. from the sea) ☎ 5268403
- PETIT PALAIS
Lungomare Marconi 54 - (panoramic location) ☎ 5265993

★★

- CRISTALLO
Gran Viale 51- (100 m. from the sea) ☎ 5265293
- SORRISO
Via Colombo 22 ☎ 5260729
- VILLA PANNONIA
Via Doge D. Michiel 48 - (historical center) ☎ 5260162
- VILLA TIZIANA
Via A. Gritti 3 ☎ 5261152

★

- GIARDINETTO
Piazzale S. M. Elisabetta 3 ☎ 5260801
- VILLA DELLE PALME
Via E. Dandolo 12 ☎ 5261312

- VILLA EDERA
Via Negroponte 13 ☎ 5260791
- AI MURAZZI
Ca' Bianca Coperti 60 ☎ 5262278
Typical setting
- BELVEDERE
P.le S. M. Elisabetta
Elegant setting - local cuisine ☎ 5260115
- DA VALENTINO
V. S. Gallo 81
Home cooking ☎ 5260128
- EXCELSIOR LIDO
L.mare Marconi 40 ☎ 5260201
Elegant setting - refined cuisine
- GRIMOD RESTAURANT
Via Gran Viale 41 - (150 m. from the sea)
Elegant setting - refined cuisine ☎ 5261945
- IL PITOSFORO
Riviera S. Nicolo 15 ☎ 5260590
Elegant setting - local cuisine
- LIBERTY RESTAURANT
L.mare Marconi 17 - (panoramic location)
Elegant setting - refined cuisine ☎ 5265921

HOTELS MESTRE

✳✳✳✳

🛏 - **AMBASCIATORI**
C.so Del Popolo 221 - (800 m. from Railroad station)   ☎ 5310699

-**ANTONY**
Via Orlanda 182 - (3 Km from the airport)   ☎ 5420022

-**SIRIO**
Via Circonvallazione 109 - (1,5 Km from Railroad station)   ☎ 984022

✳✳✳

- **AI PINI**
Via Miranese 176 - (800 m. from Railroad station)   ☎ 917722

- **CLUB HOTEL**
Via Villafranca 1 - (2 Km from highway exit)   ☎ 957722

- **DUCALE**
Via Triestina 5   ☎ 631444

- **ELITE**
Via Forte Marghera 119/A - (1500 m from the sea)   ☎ 986255

- **PARIS**
V.le Venezia 11 - (100 m from Railroad station)   ☎ 926037

✳✳

- **DELLE ROSE**
Via Millosevich 46 - (Km. 8 from Venice)   ☎ 5317711

- **PIAVE**
Via Col Moschin 10   ☎ 929477

- **SAN CARLO**
V. Forte Marghera 131- (600m. from historical center)   ☎ 970912

- **VITTORIA**
Via S. Donà 76   ☎ 616655

- **VIVIT**
P.zza Ferretto 73 - (historical center)   ☎ 951385

✳

- **ADRIA**
Via Cappuccina 34   ☎ 989755

- **DA GIACOMO**
Via Altinia 49   ☎ 631541

- **MARY**
Via Orlanda 152   ☎ 900219

- **VIDALE**
Via G.Parini 2   ☎ 5314586

- **AI VETERANI**
  P.tta Da Re 6 - (located in historical center)   ☎ 959378
  Typical setting - Local cuisine
- **AL CASON**
  Via Gatta 112 -Loc. Zelarino
  Typical setting - Local cuisine   ☎ 907907
- **BREK**
  Via Carducci 54 - (located in historical center)
  Elegant setting   ☎ 940297
- **FONTANELLA**
  Via Orlanda 4 - Loc. S. Giuliano   ☎ 5310500
  Elegant setting - refined cuisine
- **LUCY**
  Via Cimitero 14 - Loc. Compalto - (2 Km from the airport)
  Family setting - home cooking   ☎ 900748
- **OSTERIA DA MARIANO**
  Via Spalti 49
  Typical setting - Local cuisine   ☎ 615765
- **OSTERIA VECIA POSTA**
  Via Cavallotti - (500 m from Railroad station)
  Typical setting - Local cuisine   ☎ 962691
- **TINTORETTO**
  Rotatoria di Marghera   ☎ 936900
- **VALERIANO**
  Via Col di Lana 18 - (100 m from Railroad station)
  Family setting - Local cuisine   ☎ 926474
- **VENEZIA**
  Via Teatro Vecchio 5 - (located in historical center)
  Family setting - Local cuisine   ☎ 985533

★★★

- **CA' DI VALLE**
  Via Fausta 298
  ☎ 968017
- **CA' DI VALLE JUNIOR**
  C.so Italia 10
  ☎ 968123
- **FENIX**
  V. F. Baracca 45 - (50 m from the sea)
  ☎ 968040
- **HOLIDAY CENTER VALDOR**
  Via Meduna 1- Loc. Ca' Savio
  Located on the Cavallino Treporti coast
  ☎ 966108
- **LIO GRAND'HOTEL**
  P.le Lio Grando 17
  Punta Sabbioni - (located on the sea)
  ☎ 5301200
- **SOLE MARE**
  Via Fausta 345 - (100 m from the sea)
  ☎ 968023
- **UNION LIDO**
  Via Fausta 270 - (150 m from the sea)
  ☎ 968043

★★

- **AL CASON**
  C.so Europa 15/17
  (150 m from the sea)
  ☎ 968036
- **CAVALLINO BIANCO**
  V. Fausta 304
  ☎ 968018
- **FORTUNA**
  V. Fausta 313
  ☎ 968035
- **INTERNATIONAL**
  C.so Italia 15/17
  ☎ 968108
- **LA RONDINE**
  V. Fausta 60
  ☎ 966172

- **RIGHETTO**
  C.so Italia 16
  ☎ 968083

★

- **AL BUON PESCE DA ALDO**
  V. del Faro 31
  ☎ 968064
- **DA GIOVANNI**
  V. Del Faro 35
  ☎ 968063
- **LAURA**
  V. Costanziaca 3
  ☎ 5370244
- **VILLA GENTILE**
  Via Ca' Savio 25
  ☎ 5300191

RESTAURANTS

- **AL CASON**
  C.so Europa 15/17 - (300m from the sea)
  ☎ 968036
  Family setting - Home cooking
- **ALLA CHIESA**
  V. della Fonte 20/B - Loc. Ca' Ballarin
  Elegant setting - refined cuisine
  ☎ 968751
- **LAGUNA**
  V. Pordelio 444
  ☎ 968058
- **MALE'**
  Via del Granatiere 4
  (150m from the sea)
  Typical setting - Local cuisine
  ☎ 5370900
- **VALDOR**
  Via Meduna 1- Loc. Ca' Savio
  (located in historical center)
  Family setting - local cuisine
  ☎ 966108

HOTELS AND RESTAURANTS
MARGHERA

★★★★

- **FORTE AGIP**
  Rotonda Romea 1
  ☎ 936960
- **LUGANO TORRETTA**
  Via Rizzardi 11 - (500m Railroad station)
  ☎ 936777

★★★

- **COLOMBO**
  V. Paolucci 5 - (50m Railroad station)
  ☎ 920711
- **LA MAGNOLIA**
  V. della Rinascita 75
  ☎ 921267
- **LLYOD**
  Via Rizzardi 32
  ☎ 930172
- **MONDIAL**
  Via Rizzardi 21- (100 m Railroad station)
  ☎ 930099
- **VIENNA**
  Via Rizzardi 54
  ☎ 936600
- **VILLA SERENA**
  Via Mezzacapo 2/B
  ☎ 936041

★★

- **ALLA BIANCA**
  V. G.Cantore 23
  ☎ 5381125
- **COLOMBO**
  Via Grondoni, 1
  1,5 Km from highway exit
  ☎ 920711
- **PICCOLO**
  V. Trieste 2/H
  ☎ 920632
- **TOURING**
  V. Paolucci 4
  ☎ 920122

★

- **ADELE**
  P.za S. Antonio 5
  ☎ 920376
- **AMBA ALAGI**
  V. Mutilati del Lavoro 38
  ☎ 921728
- **BELVEDERE**
  V. Mezzacapo 1
  ☎ 926596
- **VILLA SERENA**
  V. F.lli Bandiera 50
  ☎ 926610

RESTAURANTS

- **AUTOESPRESSO**
  V. Fratelli Bandiera 34
  Family setting
  ☎ 930214
- **MONDIAL**
  Via Rizzardi 21 - (100 m Railroad station)
  Family setting - home cooking
  ☎ 930099
- **ROMA**
  V. C. Beccaria 11
  (1,5 km from highway exit)
  Family setting - home cooking
  ☎ 921967

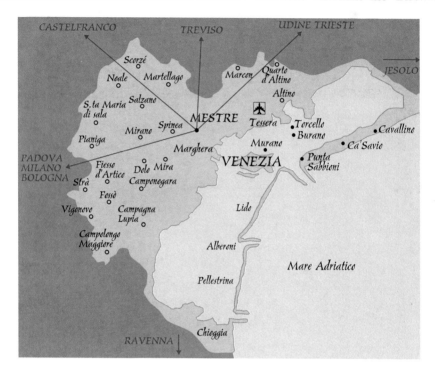

By Car

 - From the west or east: A4 Highway (Turin-Milan-Trieste)
- From the south: A13 Highway to Padua, then A4
- From the north: A27 Highway (Vittorio Veneto Mestre)

By Plane

The Marco Polo airport is located 13 km from Venice, with daily service to the main Italian and Euroepan cities. Charter flight service is also available.

To reach the city:

- By motorboat:
Lit. 15.000, one hour trip to Piazza San Marco -
Tel. 5222303

- By bus:
Bus n.5, Lit. 1.000.
Airport shuttle, Lit. 5.000, hourly arrivals in Piazzale Roma

- By motorboat-taxi:
The trip is faster, but definitely more expensive

- By train:
Venice is connected to Milan, Trieste, Bologna, Pordenone, and all of Europe.

HOSTELS IN VENICE

	ROOMS	BEDS	BATH	BREAKFAST	LUNCH	DINNER
OSTELLO DI VENEZIA Giudecca 86 ☎ 5238211 Closed from 16 January to 1 February	60	273	54	yes	yes	yes
ISTITUTO CANOSSIANO Ponte Piccolo 428 ☎ 5222157 Giudecca - Open all year	2	35	7	-	-	-
DOMUS CAVANIS Dorsoduro 912 ☎ 522826 Open from 15 June to 15 September	18	25	8	si	-	-

AGRITOURISM ESTABLISHMENTS

ENZO GELSOMINA- MAYER
via del Marinaio, 4 - Cavallino
☎ 5370431
Open from 1 April to 30 September
LA FENICE - Serafini Mario
Via Orlanda, 6 - Mestre ☎ 5420161
LE GARZETTE - Orazio Renza
Via Malamocco, 32 - Lido di Venezia
☎ 731078
Open from 5 January to 30 November

ZANELLA GABRIELLA
Via Forti, 16 - Sant' Erasmo
☎ 5285329 - Open all year
LE MANCIANE - Vianello Galdino
Via Lio Piccolo, 29 - Cavallino
☎ 658977 - Open all year

CAMPSITES IN VENICE

****

CAMPING ALBA D'ORO
Via Triestina, 214/B -
Località Cà Noghera ☎ 5415102
Restaurant - Market - Espresso Bar -
Swimming Pool - Children's play area
**

CAMPEGGIO FUSINA
Via Moranzani, 79/bis -
Località Fusina - Malcontenta
☎ 5470064 - Fax 5470050

Telex FUSINAI 411123
Market - Espresso Bar - Bazaar - Barber -
Volley Ball - Boat Rental - Children's play area
- Restaurant - Photographer - Table Tennis -
Currency Exchange - Fruits and Vegetables

CAMPEGGIO VENEZIA
Via Orlanda, 8 - Località Campalto -
Mestre - ☎ 975928
Restaurant - Market - Espresso Bar - Fruits
and Vegetables

*

CAMPEGGIO MARCO POLO
Via Triestina, 164
Località Tessera - ☎ 5415346
Restaurant - Market - Espresso Bar -
Children's play area - Game room

CAMPING JOLLY
Via A. De Marchi, 7
Località Marghera ☎ e Fax 920312
Market - Espresso Bar - Bazaar - Swimming
Pool - Canteen - Children's play area - Game
room - Table Tennis - Soccer Field - Snack
Bar - Fruits and Vegetables - Restaurant

CAMPING RIALTO
Via Orlanda, 16
Località Mestre - ☎ 900785
Market - Espresso Bar

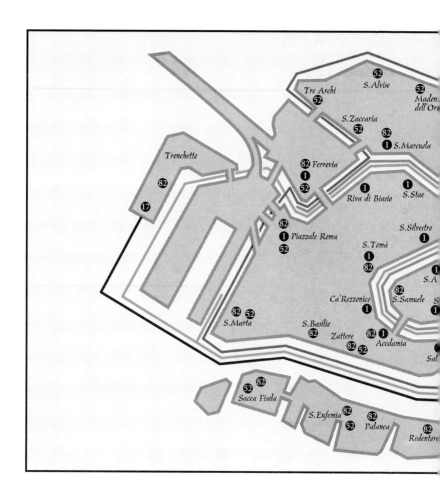

The most widely used vaporetto lines are: 1, 2, 5 and 12.

There are three types of vessels:

- the **Vaporetto**, which is slow and makes every stop along the Grand Canal.

- **Motoscafo**, which is faster and makes fewer stops along its route.

- **Motonave**, which is a big ferry and covers the longer routes.

- **Fares**
Tickets must be purchased before boarding.

A standard ticket is valid for 90 minutes.
There is a full-day ticket that can be used on all routes except 2 and 28.

Holders of "youth cards" issued by the city of Venice can obtain less expensive passes.

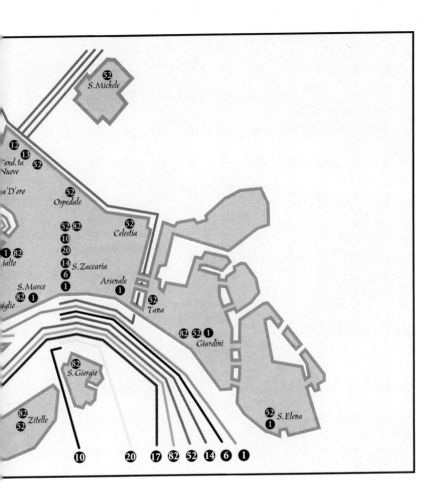

There are also cards for congress partici-pants; they are valid for eight days and entitle the holders to discounts on all routes except 2.

The "Carta Venezia" is valid for three years, and entitles the holder to discounts ranging

from 50% to 60% on all public transporta-tion. An ID photo and identification are need-ed to obtain the Carta Venezia.

For information about public transportatio̅ in Venice, contact:
- **ACTV** di Piazzale Roma (phone 5287886)
- **San Marco** (phone 780310)

- **Mestre** (phone 972073)
The line 1, 2 and 5 vaporetti go to nearly everywhere in the city, even along the Grand Canal.

INDEX OF ITINERARIES

INDEX